TEACHER'S PET PUBLICATIONS

PUZZLE PACK
for
When the Legends Die

based on the book by
Hal Borland

Written by
William T. Collins

© 2006 Teacher's Pet Publications
All Rights Reserved

The materials in this packet are copyrighted
by Teacher's Pet Publications, Inc.

These pages may be duplicated by the purchaser
for use in the purchaser's own classroom.

Copying any of these materials and distributing them
for any other purpose is a violation of the copyright laws.

© 2005 Teacher's Pet Publications, Inc.
www.tpet.com

INTRODUCTION
If you already own the LitPlan for this title, this Puzzle Pack will refresh your Unit Resource Materials and Vocabulary Resource Materials sections plus give you additional materials you can substitute into the tests. If you do not already have a complete LitPlan, these pages will give you some supplemental materials to use with your own plan. There are two main groups of materials: one set for unit words (such as characters' names, symbols, places, etc.) and one set for vocabulary words associated with the book.

WORD LIST
There is a word list for both the unit words and the vocabulary words. These lists show you which words are being used in the materials and the clues or definitions being used for those words. You may want to give students a word list with clues/definitions to help them, or you may want students to only have a word list (without clues/definitions) if you want them to work a little harder. Both are available for duplication. The word lists can also be your "calling key" for the bingo games.

FILL IN THE BLANK AND MATCHING
There are 4 each of the fill in the blank and matching worksheets for both the unit and vocabulary words. These pages can be used either as extra worksheets for students or as objective parts of a unit test. They can be done individually if students need extra help or as a whole class activity to review the material covered.

MAGIC SQUARES
The magic squares not only reinforce the material covered but also work on reasoning and math skills. Many teachers have told us that their students really enjoy doing these!

WORD SEARCH PUZZLES
The word search words go in all directions, as indicated on your answer keys. Two of the word search puzzles have the clues listed rather than the words. This makes the puzzle a little more difficult, but it reinforces the material better. Two word search puzzles have words only for students who find the clue puzzles too difficult.

CROSSWORD PUZZLES
Both unit and vocabulary word sections have 4 crossword puzzles.

BINGO CARDS
There are 32 individual bingo cards for the unit words and 32 individual bingo cards for the vocabulary words. You can use your word list as a "call list," calling the words at random and marking them off of your list as you go, or you could use the flash cards by cutting them apart and drawing the words at random from a hat (or box or whatever). To make a better review, you might ask for the definition and spelling of each word as you call it out–or you could call out the definitions and have students tell you the words they need to look for on the puzzle.

JUGGLE LETTERS
The vocabulary juggle letter game is intended to help students learn the spellings of the words. One sheet has the definitions listed on it as an extra help for students who need it or to reinforce the definitions if you choose to do so.

FLASH CARDS
We've included a set of vocabulary flash cards you can duplicate, cut, and fold for your students. Some teachers make a few sets for general use by the class; others make a set for each student. Some teachers duplicate them for each student and have the students cut & fold their own. You can cut out just the words and put them in a hat, have each student pick out one word and write the definition and a sentence for that word. Students then swap words and papers, with the next student adding a sentence of his own under the last one. You can have students swap as many times as you like. Each time the student will read the sentences written prior to his own and then add a sentence. You can cut out the words and definitions separately and play "I Have; Who Has?" Each student in the room draws a word and definition. The first student says, "I have (the name of the word). Who has the definition?" The student with the definition reads it then says, "I have (the name of the vocabulary word she has). Who has the definition?" The round continues until all words and definitions have been given.

When Legends Die Word List

No.	Word	Clue/Definition
1.	ALBERT	Mr. Left Hand
2.	ARROWS	Bows shoot them
3.	AVALANCHE	George was killed by one.
4.	BEANS	Meo grew them
5.	BEAVERFOOT	Dolly
6.	BENNY	Carpentry teacher
7.	BESSIE	Bear's Brother's mother
8.	BIT	Metal object in a horse's mouth
9.	BLACK	Thomas ___ Bull
10.	BLANKET	Bessie bought Thomas a red one.
11.	BLUE	___ Elk
12.	BORLAND	Author
13.	BROTHER	Bear's ___ (Thomas)
14.	BULL	Black ___
15.	CAMP	Cowboy's night stop
16.	CHAPS	Cowboy's leg protectors
17.	CLAW	One from a bear is long and sharp.
18.	CUB	Baby bear
19.	DEER	Bucks and does
20.	DILLON	Red's last name
21.	ELK	Deer family members
22.	GEORGE	He killed Frank No Deer.
23.	GRAYBACK	Benny's last name
24.	JIM	Store owner
25.	KNIFE	Bessie bought one for Thomas.
26.	LEFT	Albert ___ Hand
27.	LEG	Thomas broke his
28.	LEGENDS	When the ___ Die
29.	LUTHER	Thomas's roommate
30.	MARY	Nurse Redmond
31.	MEAT	Food from animals
32.	MEO	He tended his beans and peppers.
33.	NEIL	Flogged Thomas for fighting
34.	PERMITS	Papers granting permission
35.	RAIN	Water falling from the sky
36.	RED	Bet on Tom
37.	REDMOND	Nurse Mary
38.	RESERVATION	Where the Indians lived
39.	RHYTHM	Each horse had its own; beat
40.	ROOM	Luther and Thomas shared one.
41.	ROWENA	English teacher
42.	SAWMILL	Some Indians were stuck working there.
43.	SPURS	Footwear used to urge on horses
44.	STAB	Pierce flesh with a sharp object
45.	STORE	Jim owned one
46.	THATCHER	Jim's last name
47.	THOMAS	Killer Tom; Bear's Brother
48.	TRAIL	Path; place where animal was
49.	UTE	Thomas was from this Indian tribe.
50.	WALK	Tom had to learn to do it again.
51.	WOODWARD	Tom worked for him after the accident.

Copyrighted

When Legends Die Fill In The Blanks 1

_____ 1. Where the Indians lived

_____ 2. Dolly

_____ 3. Deer family members

_____ 4. Carpentry teacher

_____ 5. Food from animals

_____ 6. Pierce flesh with a sharp object

_____ 7. English teacher

_____ 8. Killer Tom; Bear's Brother

_____ 9. Benny's last name

_____ 10. He killed Frank No Deer.

_____ 11. Tom worked for him after the accident.

_____ 12. Meo grew them

_____ 13. Bet on Tom

_____ 14. Red's last name

_____ 15. Baby bear

_____ 16. One from a bear is long and sharp.

_____ 17. Papers granting permission

_____ 18. When the ___ Die

_____ 19. Thomas was from this Indian tribe.

_____ 20. Thomas broke his

When Legends Die Fill In The Blanks 1 Answer Key

RESERVATION	1. Where the Indians lived
BEAVERFOOT	2. Dolly
ELK	3. Deer family members
BENNY	4. Carpentry teacher
MEAT	5. Food from animals
STAB	6. Pierce flesh with a sharp object
ROWENA	7. English teacher
THOMAS	8. Killer Tom; Bear's Brother
GRAYBACK	9. Benny's last name
GEORGE	10. He killed Frank No Deer.
WOODWARD	11. Tom worked for him after the accident.
BEANS	12. Meo grew them
RED	13. Bet on Tom
DILLON	14. Red's last name
CUB	15. Baby bear
CLAW	16. One from a bear is long and sharp.
PERMITS	17. Papers granting permission
LEGENDS	18. When the ___ Die
UTE	19. Thomas was from this Indian tribe.
LEG	20. Thomas broke his

When Legends Die Fill In The Blanks 2

1. Luther and Thomas shared one.
2. Cowboy's leg protectors
3. Bows shoot them
4. Thomas broke his
5. Thomas ___ Bull
6. Killer Tom; Bear's Brother
7. Cowboy's night stop
8. Bear's ___ (Thomas)
9. Metal object in a horse's mouth
10. Tom worked for him after the accident.
11. Carpentry teacher
12. He killed Frank No Deer.
13. Jim's last name
14. Water falling from the sky
15. Deer family members
16. Bucks and does
17. ___ Elk
18. Nurse Redmond
19. Bessie bought one for Thomas.
20. Thomas was from this Indian tribe.

When Legends Die Fill In The Blanks 2 Answer Key

ROOM	1. Luther and Thomas shared one.
CHAPS	2. Cowboy's leg protectors
ARROWS	3. Bows shoot them
LEG	4. Thomas broke his
BLACK	5. Thomas ___ Bull
THOMAS	6. Killer Tom; Bear's Brother
CAMP	7. Cowboy's night stop
BROTHER	8. Bear's ___ (Thomas)
BIT	9. Metal object in a horse's mouth
WOODWARD	10. Tom worked for him after the accident.
BENNY	11. Carpentry teacher
GEORGE	12. He killed Frank No Deer.
THATCHER	13. Jim's last name
RAIN	14. Water falling from the sky
ELK	15. Deer family members
DEER	16. Bucks and does
BLUE	17. ___ Elk
MARY	18. Nurse Redmond
KNIFE	19. Bessie bought one for Thomas.
UTE	20. Thomas was from this Indian tribe.

When Legends Die Fill In The Blanks 3

_____ 1. Papers granting permission

_____ 2. Thomas broke his

_____ 3. Thomas's roommate

_____ 4. Bear's Brother's mother

_____ 5. Killer Tom; Bear's Brother

_____ 6. Baby bear

_____ 7. Author

_____ 8. Red's last name

_____ 9. Where the Indians lived

_____ 10. Luther and Thomas shared one.

_____ 11. Food from animals

_____ 12. Thomas was from this Indian tribe.

_____ 13. Metal object in a horse's mouth

_____ 14. Bet on Tom

_____ 15. Cowboy's leg protectors

_____ 16. Bucks and does

_____ 17. Nurse Mary

_____ 18. Mr. Left Hand

_____ 19. He killed Frank No Deer.

_____ 20. Deer family members

When Legends Die Fill In The Blanks 3 Answer Key

PERMITS	1. Papers granting permission
LEG	2. Thomas broke his
LUTHER	3. Thomas's roommate
BESSIE	4. Bear's Brother's mother
THOMAS	5. Killer Tom; Bear's Brother
CUB	6. Baby bear
BORLAND	7. Author
DILLON	8. Red's last name
RESERVATION	9. Where the Indians lived
ROOM	10. Luther and Thomas shared one.
MEAT	11. Food from animals
UTE	12. Thomas was from this Indian tribe.
BIT	13. Metal object in a horse's mouth
RED	14. Bet on Tom
CHAPS	15. Cowboy's leg protectors
DEER	16. Bucks and does
REDMOND	17. Nurse Mary
ALBERT	18. Mr. Left Hand
GEORGE	19. He killed Frank No Deer.
ELK	20. Deer family members

When Legends Die Fill In The Blanks 4

_____ 1. Deer family members

_____ 2. Bear's ___ (Thomas)

_____ 3. Bows shoot them

_____ 4. Papers granting permission

_____ 5. Albert ___ Hand

_____ 6. Pierce flesh with a sharp object

_____ 7. Jim's last name

_____ 8. When the ___ Die

_____ 9. Metal object in a horse's mouth

_____ 10. George was killed by one.

_____ 11. Bessie bought one for Thomas.

_____ 12. Where the Indians lived

_____ 13. Cowboy's leg protectors

_____ 14. Bet on Tom

_____ 15. Red's last name

_____ 16. Footwear used to urge on horses

_____ 17. Thomas was from this Indian tribe.

_____ 18. Luther and Thomas shared one.

_____ 19. English teacher

_____ 20. Thomas's roommate

When Legends Die Fill In The Blanks 4 Answer Key

ELK	1. Deer family members
BROTHER	2. Bear's ___ (Thomas)
ARROWS	3. Bows shoot them
PERMITS	4. Papers granting permission
LEFT	5. Albert ___ Hand
STAB	6. Pierce flesh with a sharp object
THATCHER	7. Jim's last name
LEGENDS	8. When the ___ Die
BIT	9. Metal object in a horse's mouth
AVALANCHE	10. George was killed by one.
KNIFE	11. Bessie bought one for Thomas.
RESERVATION	12. Where the Indians lived
CHAPS	13. Cowboy's leg protectors
RED	14. Bet on Tom
DILLON	15. Red's last name
SPURS	16. Footwear used to urge on horses
UTE	17. Thomas was from this Indian tribe.
ROOM	18. Luther and Thomas shared one.
ROWENA	19. English teacher
LUTHER	20. Thomas's roommate

When Legends Die Matching 1

___ 1. BLACK   A. Food from animals
___ 2. STAB   B. Bessie bought Thomas a red one.
___ 3. BLUE   C. Mr. Left Hand
___ 4. LEGENDS   D. Cowboy's night stop
___ 5. SPURS   E. ___ Elk
___ 6. CAMP   F. Thomas ___ Bull
___ 7. ALBERT   G. Meo grew them
___ 8. MEO   H. Pierce flesh with a sharp object
___ 9. THATCHER   I. Bessie bought one for Thomas.
___10. UTE   J. Path; place where animal was
___11. LEFT   K. Where the Indians lived
___12. TRAIL   L. Cowboy's leg protectors
___13. MARY   M. Thomas was from this Indian tribe.
___14. JIM   N. George was killed by one.
___15. BIT   O. Bet on Tom
___16. KNIFE   P. Nurse Redmond
___17. BLANKET   Q. Albert ___ Hand
___18. RESERVATION   R. Metal object in a horse's mouth
___19. CHAPS   S. He tended his beans and peppers.
___20. MEAT   T. Nurse Mary
___21. RED   U. Footwear used to urge on horses
___22. ROWENA   V. Jim's last name
___23. AVALANCHE   W. English teacher
___24. BEANS   X. When the ___ Die
___25. REDMOND   Y. Store owner

When Legends Die Matching 1 Answer Key

F - 1.	BLACK	A.	Food from animals
H - 2.	STAB	B.	Bessie bought Thomas a red one.
E - 3.	BLUE	C.	Mr. Left Hand
X - 4.	LEGENDS	D.	Cowboy's night stop
U - 5.	SPURS	E.	___ Elk
D - 6.	CAMP	F.	Thomas ___ Bull
C - 7.	ALBERT	G.	Meo grew them
S - 8.	MEO	H.	Pierce flesh with a sharp object
V - 9.	THATCHER	I.	Bessie bought one for Thomas.
M -10.	UTE	J.	Path; place where animal was
Q -11.	LEFT	K.	Where the Indians lived
J -12.	TRAIL	L.	Cowboy's leg protectors
P -13.	MARY	M.	Thomas was from this Indian tribe.
Y -14.	JIM	N.	George was killed by one.
R -15.	BIT	O.	Bet on Tom
I -16.	KNIFE	P.	Nurse Redmond
B -17.	BLANKET	Q.	Albert ___ Hand
K -18.	RESERVATION	R.	Metal object in a horse's mouth
L -19.	CHAPS	S.	He tended his beans and peppers.
A -20.	MEAT	T.	Nurse Mary
O -21.	RED	U.	Footwear used to urge on horses
W -22.	ROWENA	V.	Jim's last name
N -23.	AVALANCHE	W.	English teacher
G -24.	BEANS	X.	When the ___ Die
T -25.	REDMOND	Y.	Store owner

When Legends Die Matching 2

___ 1. THATCHER   A. Thomas's roommate
___ 2. RESERVATION   B. Jim's last name
___ 3. REDMOND   C. Baby bear
___ 4. BORLAND   D. Jim owned one
___ 5. STAB   E. Thomas broke his
___ 6. DILLON   F. Some Indians were stuck working there.
___ 7. KNIFE   G. Thomas was from this Indian tribe.
___ 8. JIM   H. Author
___ 9. LUTHER   I. George was killed by one.
___ 10. LEG   J. Bear's ___ (Thomas)
___ 11. AVALANCHE   K. Nurse Redmond
___ 12. MARY   L. Food from animals
___ 13. LEGENDS   M. Nurse Mary
___ 14. ARROWS   N. Bessie bought one for Thomas.
___ 15. STORE   O. One from a bear is long and sharp.
___ 16. MEAT   P. English teacher
___ 17. UTE   Q. Pierce flesh with a sharp object
___ 18. BROTHER   R. When the ___ Die
___ 19. TRAIL   S. Red's last name
___ 20. CUB   T. Where the Indians lived
___ 21. ROWENA   U. Path; place where animal was
___ 22. CLAW   V. Bows shoot them
___ 23. BIT   W. Metal object in a horse's mouth
___ 24. SAWMILL   X. Footwear used to urge on horses
___ 25. SPURS   Y. Store owner

When Legends Die Matching 2 Answer Key

B - 1.	THATCHER	A.	Thomas's roommate
T - 2.	RESERVATION	B.	Jim's last name
M - 3.	REDMOND	C.	Baby bear
H - 4.	BORLAND	D.	Jim owned one
Q - 5.	STAB	E.	Thomas broke his
S - 6.	DILLON	F.	Some Indians were stuck working there.
N - 7.	KNIFE	G.	Thomas was from this Indian tribe.
Y - 8.	JIM	H.	Author
A - 9.	LUTHER	I.	George was killed by one.
E - 10.	LEG	J.	Bear's ___ (Thomas)
I - 11.	AVALANCHE	K.	Nurse Redmond
K - 12.	MARY	L.	Food from animals
R - 13.	LEGENDS	M.	Nurse Mary
V - 14.	ARROWS	N.	Bessie bought one for Thomas.
D - 15.	STORE	O.	One from a bear is long and sharp.
L - 16.	MEAT	P.	English teacher
G - 17.	UTE	Q.	Pierce flesh with a sharp object
J - 18.	BROTHER	R.	When the ___ Die
U - 19.	TRAIL	S.	Red's last name
C - 20.	CUB	T.	Where the Indians lived
P - 21.	ROWENA	U.	Path; place where animal was
O - 22.	CLAW	V.	Bows shoot them
W - 23.	BIT	W.	Metal object in a horse's mouth
F - 24.	SAWMILL	X.	Footwear used to urge on horses
X - 25.	SPURS	Y.	Store owner

When Legends Die Matching 3

___ 1. AVALANCHE   A. Bows shoot them
___ 2. THATCHER   B. George was killed by one.
___ 3. WALK   C. Thomas was from this Indian tribe.
___ 4. REDMOND   D. Thomas ___ Bull
___ 5. CAMP   E. Mr. Left Hand
___ 6. SAWMILL   F. Nurse Mary
___ 7. BEAVERFOOT   G. He killed Frank No Deer.
___ 8. TRAIL   H. Some Indians were stuck working there.
___ 9. BLACK   I. Bucks and does
___ 10. ROOM   J. Where the Indians lived
___ 11. DILLON   K. Meo grew them
___ 12. GRAYBACK   L. Path; place where animal was
___ 13. GEORGE   M. Benny's last name
___ 14. BEANS   N. Author
___ 15. MEO   O. Luther and Thomas shared one.
___ 16. RAIN   P. Cowboy's leg protectors
___ 17. ALBERT   Q. Jim owned one
___ 18. RESERVATION   R. Water falling from the sky
___ 19. BORLAND   S. Dolly
___ 20. UTE   T. Cowboy's night stop
___ 21. STORE   U. Red's last name
___ 22. DEER   V. He tended his beans and peppers.
___ 23. CHAPS   W. Bessie bought Thomas a red one.
___ 24. BLANKET   X. Tom had to learn to do it again.
___ 25. ARROWS   Y. Jim's last name

When Legends Die Matching 3 Answer Key

B -	1. AVALANCHE	A.	Bows shoot them
Y -	2. THATCHER	B.	George was killed by one.
X -	3. WALK	C.	Thomas was from this Indian tribe.
F -	4. REDMOND	D.	Thomas ___ Bull
T -	5. CAMP	E.	Mr. Left Hand
H -	6. SAWMILL	F.	Nurse Mary
S -	7. BEAVERFOOT	G.	He killed Frank No Deer.
L -	8. TRAIL	H.	Some Indians were stuck working there.
D -	9. BLACK	I.	Bucks and does
O -	10. ROOM	J.	Where the Indians lived
U -	11. DILLON	K.	Meo grew them
M -	12. GRAYBACK	L.	Path; place where animal was
G -	13. GEORGE	M.	Benny's last name
K -	14. BEANS	N.	Author
V -	15. MEO	O.	Luther and Thomas shared one.
R -	16. RAIN	P.	Cowboy's leg protectors
E -	17. ALBERT	Q.	Jim owned one
J -	18. RESERVATION	R.	Water falling from the sky
N -	19. BORLAND	S.	Dolly
C -	20. UTE	T.	Cowboy's night stop
Q -	21. STORE	U.	Red's last name
I -	22. DEER	V.	He tended his beans and peppers.
P -	23. CHAPS	W.	Bessie bought Thomas a red one.
W -	24. BLANKET	X.	Tom had to learn to do it again.
A -	25. ARROWS	Y.	Jim's last name

When Legends Die Matching 4

___ 1. MEO   A. Killer Tom; Bear's Brother
___ 2. DILLON   B. Cowboy's night stop
___ 3. MEAT   C. Black ___
___ 4. SAWMILL   D. When the ___ Die
___ 5. BULL   E. Food from animals
___ 6. UTE   F. Baby bear
___ 7. GEORGE   G. Tom had to learn to do it again.
___ 8. THOMAS   H. Mr. Left Hand
___ 9. BORLAND   I. Bessie bought Thomas a red one.
___10. CAMP   J. Store owner
___11. CUB   K. He killed Frank No Deer.
___12. JIM   L. Metal object in a horse's mouth
___13. KNIFE   M. Thomas was from this Indian tribe.
___14. NEIL   N. Jim's last name
___15. CHAPS   O. Bet on Tom
___16. LEGENDS   P. Some Indians were stuck working there.
___17. RED   Q. Thomas ___ Bull
___18. ELK   R. Cowboy's leg protectors
___19. BLACK   S. He tended his beans and peppers.
___20. STORE   T. Bessie bought one for Thomas.
___21. THATCHER   U. Red's last name
___22. BIT   V. Flogged Thomas for fighting
___23. ALBERT   W. Author
___24. BLANKET   X. Deer family members
___25. WALK   Y. Jim owned one

When Legends Die Matching 4 Answer Key

S - 1.	MEO	A.	Killer Tom; Bear's Brother
U - 2.	DILLON	B.	Cowboy's night stop
E - 3.	MEAT	C.	Black ___
P - 4.	SAWMILL	D.	When the ___ Die
C - 5.	BULL	E.	Food from animals
M - 6.	UTE	F.	Baby bear
K - 7.	GEORGE	G.	Tom had to learn to do it again.
A - 8.	THOMAS	H.	Mr. Left Hand
W - 9.	BORLAND	I.	Bessie bought Thomas a red one.
B - 10.	CAMP	J.	Store owner
F - 11.	CUB	K.	He killed Frank No Deer.
J - 12.	JIM	L.	Metal object in a horse's mouth
T - 13.	KNIFE	M.	Thomas was from this Indian tribe.
V - 14.	NEIL	N.	Jim's last name
R - 15.	CHAPS	O.	Bet on Tom
D - 16.	LEGENDS	P.	Some Indians were stuck working there.
O - 17.	RED	Q.	Thomas ___ Bull
X - 18.	ELK	R.	Cowboy's leg protectors
Q - 19.	BLACK	S.	He tended his beans and peppers.
Y - 20.	STORE	T.	Bessie bought one for Thomas.
N - 21.	THATCHER	U.	Red's last name
L - 22.	BIT	V.	Flogged Thomas for fighting
H - 23.	ALBERT	W.	Author
I - 24.	BLANKET	X.	Deer family members
G - 25.	WALK	Y.	Jim owned one

When Legends Die Magic Squares 1

Match the definition with the vocabulary word. Put your answers in the magic squares below. When your answers are correct, all columns and rows will add to the same number.

A. KNIFE   E. SAWMILL   I. GRAYBACK   M. STORE
B. BEAVERFOOT   F. PERMITS   J. WALK   N. BULL
C. RAIN   G. ROWENA   K. WOODWARD   O. NEIL
D. UTE   H. BLUE   L. RESERVATION P. LEFT

1. ___ Elk
2. Bessie bought one for Thomas.
3. Dolly
4. English teacher
5. Tom had to learn to do it again.
6. Flogged Thomas for fighting
7. Albert ___ Hand
8. Benny's last name
9. Tom worked for him after the accident.
10. Black ___
11. Jim owned one
12. Where the Indians lived
13. Some Indians were stuck working there.
14. Thomas was from this Indian tribe.
15. Water falling from the sky
16. Papers granting permission

A=	B=	C=	D=
E=	F=	G=	H=
I=	J=	K=	L=
M=	N=	O=	P=

When Legends Die Magic Squares 1 Answer Key

Match the definition with the vocabulary word. Put your answers in the magic squares below. When your answers are correct, all columns and rows will add to the same number.

A. KNIFE   E. SAWMILL   I. GRAYBACK   M. STORE
B. BEAVERFOOT   F. PERMITS   J. WALK   N. BULL
C. RAIN   G. ROWENA   K. WOODWARD   O. NEIL
D. UTE   H. BLUE   L. RESERVATION   P. LEFT

1. ___ Elk
2. Bessie bought one for Thomas.
3. Dolly
4. English teacher
5. Tom had to learn to do it again.
6. Flogged Thomas for fighting
7. Albert ___ Hand
8. Benny's last name
9. Tom worked for him after the accident.
10. Black ___
11. Jim owned one
12. Where the Indians lived
13. Some Indians were stuck working there.
14. Thomas was from this Indian tribe.
15. Water falling from the sky
16. Papers granting permission

A=2	B=3	C=15	D=14
E=13	F=16	G=4	H=1
I=8	J=5	K=9	L=12
M=11	N=10	O=6	P=7

When Legends Die Magic Squares 2

Match the definition with the vocabulary word. Put your answers in the magic squares below. When your answers are correct, all columns and rows will add to the same number.

A. GEORGE
B. REDMOND
C. DEER
D. THATCHER
E. CAMP
F. RAIN
G. BORLAND
H. BLANKET
I. LEGENDS
J. LEG
K. WALK
L. TRAIL
M. STORE
N. PERMITS
O. ROWENA
P. BEANS

1. Nurse Mary
2. Author
3. Tom had to learn to do it again.
4. Papers granting permission
5. Jim owned one
6. Path; place where animal was
7. Bessie bought Thomas a red one.
8. He killed Frank No Deer.
9. Meo grew them
10. When the ___ Die
11. Cowboy's night stop
12. Jim's last name
13. Bucks and does
14. Water falling from the sky
15. Thomas broke his
16. English teacher

A=	B=	C=	D=
E=	F=	G=	H=
I=	J=	K=	L=
M=	N=	O=	P=

When Legends Die Magic Squares 2 Answer Key

Match the definition with the vocabulary word. Put your answers in the magic squares below. When your answers are correct, all columns and rows will add to the same number.

A. GEORGE   E. CAMP   I. LEGENDS   M. STORE
B. REDMOND   F. RAIN   J. LEG   N. PERMITS
C. DEER   G. BORLAND   K. WALK   O. ROWENA
D. THATCHER   H. BLANKET   L. TRAIL   P. BEANS

1. Nurse Mary
2. Author
3. Tom had to learn to do it again.
4. Papers granting permission
5. Jim owned one
6. Path; place where animal was
7. Bessie bought Thomas a red one.
8. He killed Frank No Deer.
9. Meo grew them
10. When the ___ Die
11. Cowboy's night stop
12. Jim's last name
13. Bucks and does
14. Water falling from the sky
15. Thomas broke his
16. English teacher

A=8	B=1	C=13	D=12
E=11	F=14	G=2	H=7
I=10	J=15	K=3	L=6
M=5	N=4	O=16	P=9

When Legends Die Magic Squares 3

Match the definition with the vocabulary word. Put your answers in the magic squares below. When your answers are correct, all columns and rows will add to the same number.

A. BIT
B. REDMOND
C. CAMP
D. LEGENDS
E. MEAT
F. THOMAS
G. BLANKET
H. CLAW
I. AVALANCHE
J. BLUE
K. ROOM
L. MARY
M. NEIL
N. PERMITS
O. RHYTHM
P. MEO

1. One from a bear is long and sharp.
2. Metal object in a horse's mouth
3. Nurse Mary
4. Bessie bought Thomas a red one.
5. ___ Elk
6. Each horse had its own; beat
7. He tended his beans and peppers.
8. George was killed by one.
9. Luther and Thomas shared one.
10. Papers granting permission
11. Flogged Thomas for fighting
12. Nurse Redmond
13. Food from animals
14. When the ___ Die
15. Cowboy's night stop
16. Killer Tom; Bear's Brother

A=	B=	C=	D=
E=	F=	G=	H=
I=	J=	K=	L=
M=	N=	O=	P=

When Legends Die Magic Squares 3 Answer Key

Match the definition with the vocabulary word. Put your answers in the magic squares below. When your answers are correct, all columns and rows will add to the same number.

A. BIT   E. MEAT   I. AVALANCHE   M. NEIL
B. REDMOND   F. THOMAS   J. BLUE   N. PERMITS
C. CAMP   G. BLANKET   K. ROOM   O. RHYTHM
D. LEGENDS   H. CLAW   L. MARY   P. MEO

1. One from a bear is long and sharp.
2. Metal object in a horse's mouth
3. Nurse Mary
4. Bessie bought Thomas a red one.
5. ___ Elk
6. Each horse had its own; beat
7. He tended his beans and peppers.
8. George was killed by one.
9. Luther and Thomas shared one.
10. Papers granting permission
11. Flogged Thomas for fighting
12. Nurse Redmond
13. Food from animals
14. When the ___ Die
15. Cowboy's night stop
16. Killer Tom; Bear's Brother

A=2	B=3	C=15	D=14
E=13	F=16	G=4	H=1
I=8	J=5	K=9	L=12
M=11	N=10	O=6	P=7

Copyrighted

When Legends Die Magic Squares 4

Match the definition with the vocabulary word. Put your answers in the magic squares below. When your answers are correct, all columns and rows will add to the same number.

A. RED
B. JIM
C. MEAT
D. MARY
E. LEGENDS
F. AVALANCHE
G. BIT
H. TRAIL
I. WALK
J. PERMITS
K. GRAYBACK
L. DILLON
M. THATCHER
N. RAIN
O. SPURS
P. CHAPS

1. Food from animals
2. Papers granting permission
3. George was killed by one.
4. Footwear used to urge on horses
5. Cowboy's leg protectors
6. When the ___ Die
7. Tom had to learn to do it again.
8. Nurse Redmond
9. Jim's last name
10. Path; place where animal was
11. Red's last name
12. Bet on Tom
13. Store owner
14. Benny's last name
15. Metal object in a horse's mouth
16. Water falling from the sky

A=	B=	C=	D=
E=	F=	G=	H=
I=	J=	K=	L=
M=	N=	O=	P=

When Legends Die Magic Squares 4 Answer Key

Match the definition with the vocabulary word. Put your answers in the magic squares below. When your answers are correct, all columns and rows will add to the same number.

A. RED
B. JIM
C. MEAT
D. MARY
E. LEGENDS
F. AVALANCHE
G. BIT
H. TRAIL
I. WALK
J. PERMITS
K. GRAYBACK
L. DILLON
M. THATCHER
N. RAIN
O. SPURS
P. CHAPS

1. Food from animals
2. Papers granting permission
3. George was killed by one.
4. Footwear used to urge on horses
5. Cowboy's leg protectors
6. When the ___ Die
7. Tom had to learn to do it again.
8. Nurse Redmond
9. Jim's last name
10. Path; place where animal was
11. Red's last name
12. Bet on Tom
13. Store owner
14. Benny's last name
15. Metal object in a horse's mouth
16. Water falling from the sky

A=12	B=13	C=1	D=8
E=6	F=3	G=15	H=10
I=7	J=2	K=14	L=11
M=9	N=16	O=4	P=5

When Legends Die Word Search 1

Words are placed backwards, forward, diagonally, up and down. Clues listed below can help you find the words. Circle the hidden vocabulary words in the maze.

```
B A T S T Z M B B F A Y P R H Y T H M X
E M Q F B J G L L E S R E T E D J W Q S
A N E D D S Y A U D S P R M D D Q Z T W
N L M G J P X N T K V S M O F J M M Q F
S C L A W N L K H F M K I W W H S O F W
P V V D O X C E E Y F X T E X S D P N B
S P H L T A C T R T J W S X Q H N F H D
M S L H B R L J O E T W Y W L M E D D M
T I Q Y Q N T O G Q D R H Z T B G B J P
D B A X L B F R C C S C N B C I E D S G
X R B K S R O C X H A L B E R T L H A P
G O S T E E P J H J B L V C U W R R W D
H T S V G V M X B A K F J C E P B A M C
D H A T B R B E L L P R B I U L B S I C
L E G W O O D W A R D S O E M B K P L L
B R E M R R V W C T E J F W N N C U L J
W X O R L R E T K X R I E C E N G R M Q
Y O T H A T C H E R N T U I A N Y S A L
R L T I N F R J V K N X L F X M A Q R Y
K T N P D T H O M A S N B U L L P K Y Z
```

Albert ___ Hand (4)
Author (7)
Baby bear (3)
Bear's Brother's mother (6)
Bear's ___ (Thomas) (7)
Benny's last name (8)
Bessie bought Thomas a red one. (7)
Bessie bought one for Thomas. (5)
Bet on Tom (3)
Black ___ (4)
Bows shoot them (6)
Bucks and does (4)
Carpentry teacher (5)
Cowboy's leg protectors (5)
Cowboy's night stop (4)
Deer family members (3)
Dolly (10)
Each horse had its own; beat (6)
English teacher (6)
Flogged Thomas for fighting (4)
Food from animals (4)
Footwear used to urge on horses (5)
He killed Frank No Deer. (6)
He tended his beans and peppers. (3)
Jim owned one (5)

Jim's last name (8)
Killer Tom; Bear's Brother (6)
Luther and Thomas shared one. (4)
Meo grew them (5)
Metal object in a horse's mouth (3)
Mr. Left Hand (6)
Nurse Mary (7)
Nurse Redmond (4)
One from a bear is long and sharp. (4)
Papers granting permission (7)
Path; place where animal was (5)
Pierce flesh with a sharp object (4)
Red's last name (6)
Some Indians were stuck working there. (7)
Store owner (3)
Thomas ___ Bull (5)
Thomas broke his (3)
Thomas was from this Indian tribe. (3)
Thomas's roommate (6)
Tom had to learn to do it again. (4)
Tom worked for him after the accident. (8)
Water falling from the sky (4)
When the ___ Die (7)
___ Elk (4)

When Legends Die Word Search 1 Answer Key

Words are placed backwards, forward, diagonally, up and down. Clues listed below can help you find the words. Circle the hidden vocabulary words in the maze.

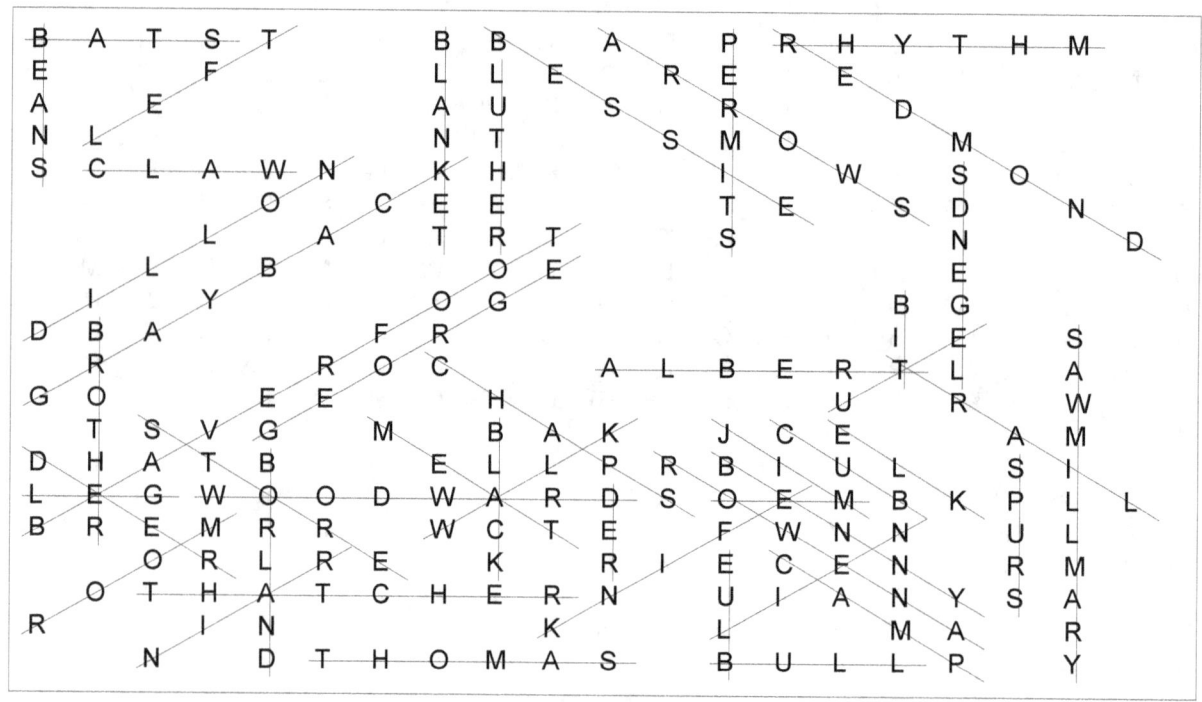

Albert ___ Hand (4)
Author (7)
Baby bear (3)
Bear's Brother's mother (6)
Bear's ___ (Thomas) (7)
Benny's last name (8)
Bessie bought Thomas a red one. (7)
Bessie bought one for Thomas. (5)
Bet on Tom (3)
Black ___ (4)
Bows shoot them (6)
Bucks and does (4)
Carpentry teacher (5)
Cowboy's leg protectors (5)
Cowboy's night stop (4)
Deer family members (3)
Dolly (10)
Each horse had its own; beat (6)
English teacher (6)
Flogged Thomas for fighting (4)
Food from animals (4)
Footwear used to urge on horses (5)
He killed Frank No Deer. (6)
He tended his beans and peppers. (3)
Jim owned one (5)

Jim's last name (8)
Killer Tom; Bear's Brother (6)
Luther and Thomas shared one. (4)
Meo grew them (5)
Metal object in a horse's mouth (3)
Mr. Left Hand (6)
Nurse Mary (7)
Nurse Redmond (4)
One from a bear is long and sharp. (4)
Papers granting permission (7)
Path; place where animal was (5)
Pierce flesh with a sharp object (4)
Red's last name (6)
Some Indians were stuck working there. (7)
Store owner (3)
Thomas ___ Bull (5)
Thomas broke his (3)
Thomas was from this Indian tribe. (3)
Thomas's roommate (6)
Tom had to learn to do it again. (4)
Tom worked for him after the accident. (8)
Water falling from the sky (4)
When the ___ Die (7)
___ Elk (4)

When Legends Die Word Search 2

Words are placed backwards, forward, diagonally, up and down. Clues listed below can help you find the words. Circle the hidden vocabulary words in the maze.

```
A L B E R T G Q G H H P K N I F E L L H
V C B R C C Y N R T B E N N Y C L I N D
G C E H T F X L A M N R N T M I A V N Z
L Y A D M H D Y Y R T M H Y M R N O B Z
M H V K B Z A Q B B Y I P W T T M N E Z
W R E L C K G T A K E T A L F D F S A B
Y R R J J Y T C N L S D N E G E L N B
N S F R S E Y A K H B V S R L G F O S T
Y B O F R J L S C R E Q M I R B I D V J
B V O O K B L M U N K R R O E T C R T K
S Z T E K N A L B L U E E P A C H A P S
B S N Q S J K A Z I H G D V R A R W B T
D L G R K N T C N T T N R B R M O D H X
K S U R N S K M U P M E E O O P O O R S
B P M E O R I L T Y S Q H R W W M O A W
S H S J L J W A C E C J T L S A R W I P
L N L G L M E E R R L M O A S L B Z N X
N E I L I M V L X B A X R N U K D U R F
S L Y C D X R K N R W N B D T Y H V L Y
R O W E N A R H Y T H M D E E R C T S L
```

Albert ___ Hand (4)
Author (7)
Baby bear (3)
Bear's Brother's mother (6)
Bear's ___ (Thomas) (7)
Benny's last name (8)
Bessie bought Thomas a red one. (7)
Bessie bought one for Thomas. (5)
Bet on Tom (3)
Black ___ (4)
Bows shoot them (6)
Bucks and does (4)
Carpentry teacher (5)
Cowboy's leg protectors (5)
Cowboy's night stop (4)
Deer family members (3)
Dolly (10)
Each horse had its own; beat (6)
English teacher (6)
Flogged Thomas for fighting (4)
Food from animals (4)
Footwear used to urge on horses (5)
He killed Frank No Deer. (6)
He tended his beans and peppers. (3)
Jim owned one (5)

Jim's last name (8)
Killer Tom; Bear's Brother (6)
Luther and Thomas shared one. (4)
Meo grew them (5)
Metal object in a horse's mouth (3)
Mr. Left Hand (6)
Nurse Mary (7)
Nurse Redmond (4)
One from a bear is long and sharp. (4)
Papers granting permission (7)
Path; place where animal was (5)
Pierce flesh with a sharp object (4)
Red's last name (6)
Some Indians were stuck working there. (7)
Store owner (3)
Thomas ___ Bull (5)
Thomas broke his (3)
Thomas was from this Indian tribe. (3)
Thomas's roommate (6)
Tom had to learn to do it again. (4)
Tom worked for him after the accident. (8)
Water falling from the sky (4)
When the ___ Die (7)
Where the Indians lived (11)
___ Elk (4)

When Legends Die Word Search 2 Answer Key

Words are placed backwards, forward, diagonally, up and down. Clues listed below can help you find the words. Circle the hidden vocabulary words in the maze.

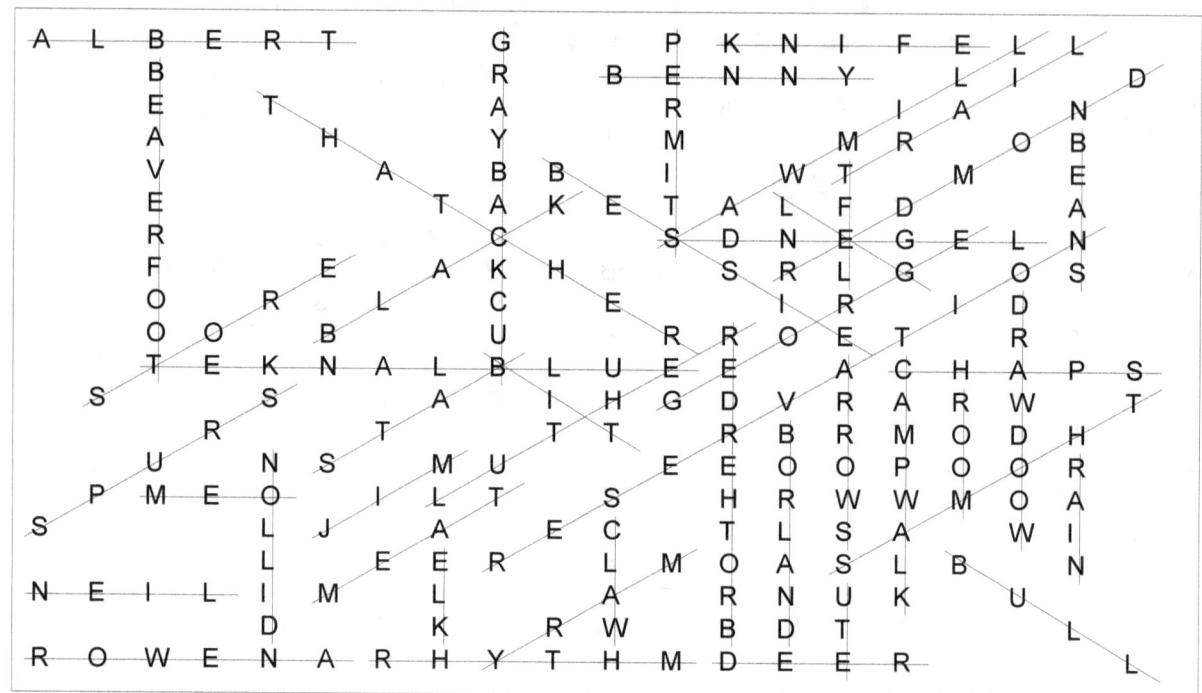

Albert ___ Hand (4)
Author (7)
Baby bear (3)
Bear's Brother's mother (6)
Bear's ___ (Thomas) (7)
Benny's last name (8)
Bessie bought Thomas a red one. (7)
Bessie bought one for Thomas. (5)
Bet on Tom (3)
Black ___ (4)
Bows shoot them (6)
Bucks and does (4)
Carpentry teacher (5)
Cowboy's leg protectors (5)
Cowboy's night stop (4)
Deer family members (3)
Dolly (10)
Each horse had its own; beat (6)
English teacher (6)
Flogged Thomas for fighting (4)
Food from animals (4)
Footwear used to urge on horses (5)
He killed Frank No Deer. (6)
He tended his beans and peppers. (3)
Jim owned one (5)

Jim's last name (8)
Killer Tom; Bear's Brother (6)
Luther and Thomas shared one. (4)
Meo grew them (5)
Metal object in a horse's mouth (3)
Mr. Left Hand (6)
Nurse Mary (7)
Nurse Redmond (4)
One from a bear is long and sharp. (4)
Papers granting permission (7)
Path; place where animal was (5)
Pierce flesh with a sharp object (4)
Red's last name (6)
Some Indians were stuck working there. (7)
Store owner (3)
Thomas ___ Bull (5)
Thomas broke his (3)
Thomas was from this Indian tribe. (3)
Thomas's roommate (6)
Tom had to learn to do it again. (4)
Tom worked for him after the accident. (8)
Water falling from the sky (4)
When the ___ Die (7)
Where the Indians lived (11)
___ Elk (4)

When Legends Die Word Search 3

Words are placed backwards, forward, diagonally, up and down. Words listed below are included in the maze. Circle the hidden vocabulary words in the maze.

```
Z P X D W A V A L A N C H E G R O E G D
W E J S O L G R E S E R V A T I O N H P
S R K Q O V J C D Z P T S W O R R A P Q
N M T R D R D T X I W F S J C E D B X S
E I Y T W N H B V R L E P E V H A E R H
I T S X A B K T R A I L T H A T C H E R
S S G L R G W G Y K E U O X S U K U D R
S K R N D X G G S G M Q O N M L L W X
E O T G C G N Y E K E H F Z D B R G P S
B R O T H E R N R O O M R N I A R B S K
Y E A C C P D A V B B Z E M E Z T P A M
B E A W L S R K Y C G S V A X I A F W K
M E T N Q A O M F B C Z A R V H L S M M
Q G N H S N W J P M A C E Y C B R C I Z
X M T N O R E M H L C C B P T U H J L K
M J V B Y M N X B T H U K N P S Y M L X
W G E L Q P A E F I N K B S R D T E C H
C A C A M J R S T C G U I D S B H O X K
C S L C Y T N G V R L Y T N H D M G R C
X N G K T E K N A L B R E D M O N D X E
```

ALBERT	BORLAND	GRAYBACK	PERMITS	STORE
ARROWS	BROTHER	JIM	RAIN	THATCHER
AVALANCHE	BULL	KNIFE	RED	THOMAS
BEANS	CAMP	LEFT	REDMOND	TRAIL
BEAVERFOOT	CHAPS	LEG	RESERVATION	UTE
BENNY	CLAW	LEGENDS	RHYTHM	WALK
BESSIE	CUB	LUTHER	ROOM	WOODWARD
BIT	DEER	MARY	ROWENA	
BLACK	DILLON	MEAT	SAWMILL	
BLANKET	ELK	MEO	SPURS	
BLUE	GEORGE	NEIL	STAB	

When Legends Die Word Search 3 Answer Key

Words are placed backwards, forward, diagonally, up and down. Words listed below are included in the maze. Circle the hidden vocabulary words in the maze.

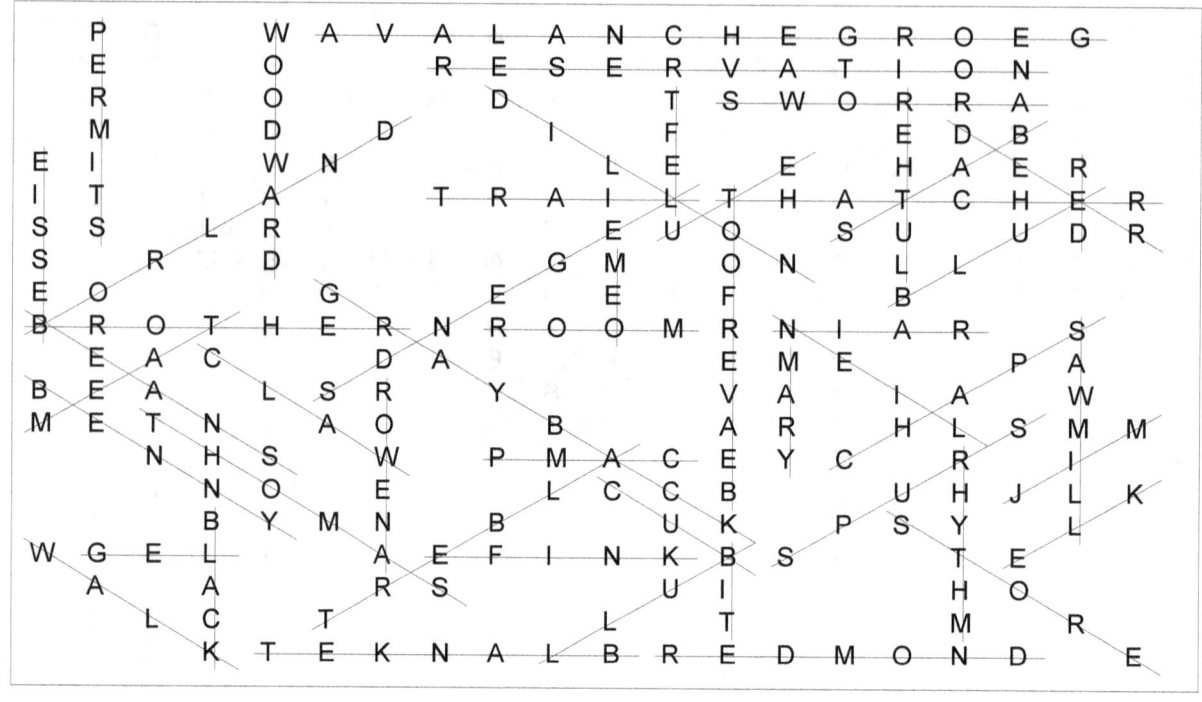

ALBERT	BORLAND	GRAYBACK	PERMITS	STORE
ARROWS	BROTHER	JIM	RAIN	THATCHER
AVALANCHE	BULL	KNIFE	RED	THOMAS
BEANS	CAMP	LEFT	REDMOND	TRAIL
BEAVERFOOT	CHAPS	LEG	RESERVATION	UTE
BENNY	CLAW	LEGENDS	RHYTHM	WALK
BESSIE	CUB	LUTHER	ROOM	WOODWARD
BIT	DEER	MARY	ROWENA	
BLACK	DILLON	MEAT	SAWMILL	
BLANKET	ELK	MEO	SPURS	
BLUE	GEORGE	NEIL	STAB	

When Legends Die Word Search 4

Words are placed backwards, forward, diagonally, up and down. Words listed below are included in the maze. Circle the hidden vocabulary words in the maze.

```
B R O T H E R K K Z B N F Z C L A W Y B
E H A V A L A N C H E T X J P S T W M S
A F Y X Y Q F I X H S H B Z G T M N X L
V X D S Q R D F L X S O C R W I G F Y K
E D V P G K V E E Y I M Z T T M H N B H
R R N H J J J V F Z E A Y R B R N P A T
F M K K W M E A T M M S T O R E L K T T
O K C A B Y A R G R W A A M B P A E S L
O F B G F B E S N O Q N R W J V K N F P
T C U B N B N N R E E D N Y M N D Y S L
J T H X L L U R X T I K M Y A I G P B Y
T G R A D U A L S U C L E L L K L K I D
L H C P P E W A L K R G B L L G R L T M
L K A J F S X B E N R G O V E C E R R L
Z T G T H V R S G O B N C L A X D C A T
P Q Y K C B E X E Y X M A W N Q M Y I D
R A I N T H D G N R O O M M E O O Y L L
S P U R S R E B D C C I P L W Y N R H S
L U T H E R C R S B J W M R O D D D T G
W O O D W A R D N A L R O B R H Y T H M
```

ALBERT	BLUE	ELK	MEAT	SAWMILL
ARROWS	BORLAND	GEORGE	MEO	SPURS
AVALANCHE	BROTHER	GRAYBACK	NEIL	STAB
BEANS	BULL	JIM	PERMITS	STORE
BEAVERFOOT	CAMP	KNIFE	RAIN	THATCHER
BENNY	CHAPS	LEFT	RED	THOMAS
BESSIE	CLAW	LEG	REDMOND	TRAIL
BIT	CUB	LEGENDS	RHYTHM	UTE
BLACK	DEER	LUTHER	ROOM	WALK
BLANKET	DILLON	MARY	ROWENA	WOODWARD

When Legends Die Word Search 4 Answer Key

Words are placed backwards, forward, diagonally, up and down. Words listed below are included in the maze. Circle the hidden vocabulary words in the maze.

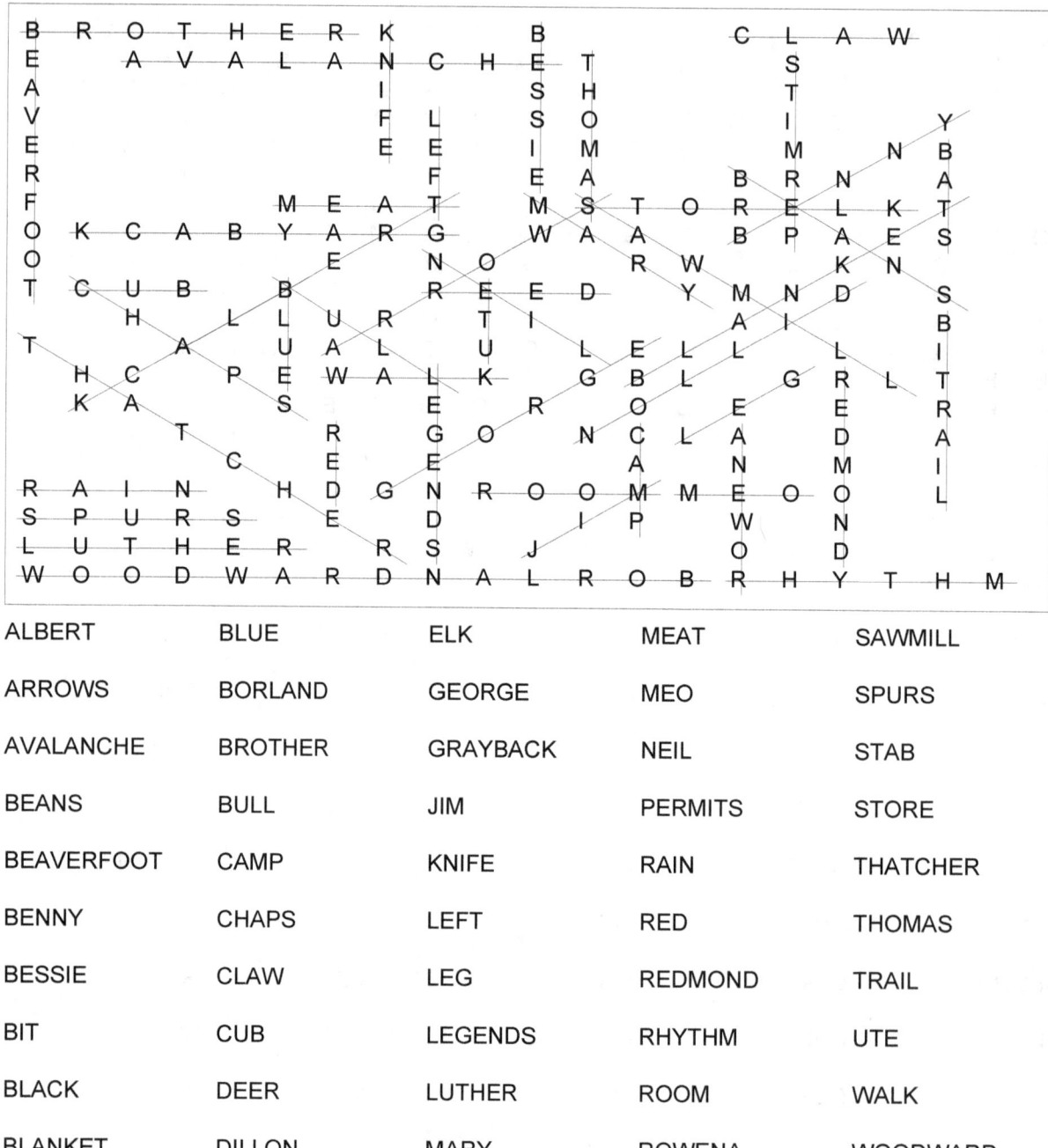

ALBERT	BLUE	ELK	MEAT	SAWMILL
ARROWS	BORLAND	GEORGE	MEO	SPURS
AVALANCHE	BROTHER	GRAYBACK	NEIL	STAB
BEANS	BULL	JIM	PERMITS	STORE
BEAVERFOOT	CAMP	KNIFE	RAIN	THATCHER
BENNY	CHAPS	LEFT	RED	THOMAS
BESSIE	CLAW	LEG	REDMOND	TRAIL
BIT	CUB	LEGENDS	RHYTHM	UTE
BLACK	DEER	LUTHER	ROOM	WALK
BLANKET	DILLON	MARY	ROWENA	WOODWARD

When Legends Die Crossword 1

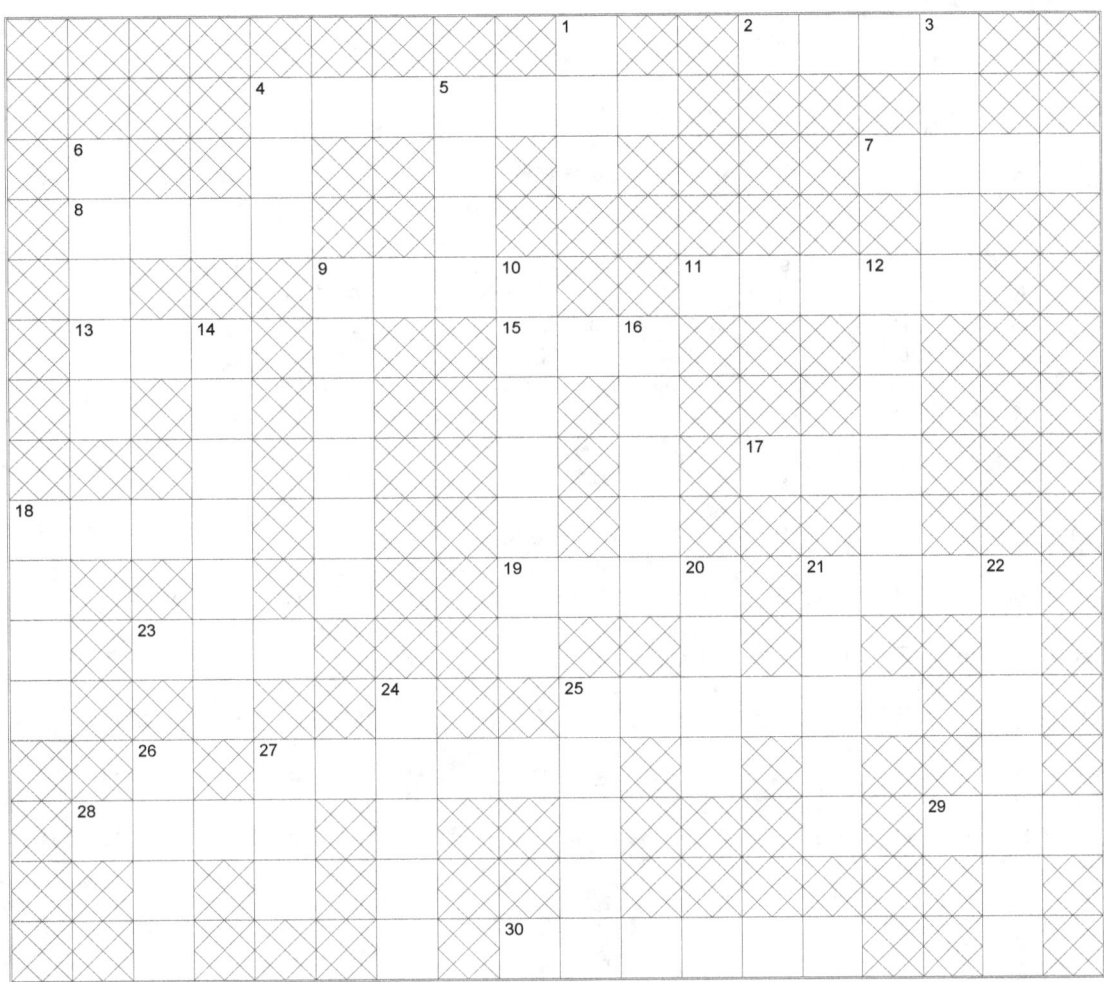

Across
2. Pierce flesh with a sharp object
4. Bessie bought Thomas a red one.
7. Tom had to learn to do it again.
8. Albert ___ Hand
9. Black ___
11. Footwear used to urge on horses
13. Baby bear
15. Deer family members
17. Thomas was from this Indian tribe.
18. Food from animals
19. Bucks and does
21. Cowboy's night stop
23. Bet on Tom
25. Killer Tom; Bear's Brother
27. Thomas's roommate
28. ___ Elk
29. Store owner
30. Mr. Left Hand

Down
1. He tended his beans and peppers.
3. Meo grew them
4. Metal object in a horse's mouth
5. Flogged Thomas for fighting
6. Thomas ___ Bull
9. Bear's Brother's mother
10. When the ___ Die
12. English teacher
14. Bear's ___ (Thomas)
16. Bessie bought one for Thomas.
18. Nurse Redmond
20. Luther and Thomas shared one.
21. Cowboy's leg protectors
22. Papers granting permission
24. Jim owned one
25. Path; place where animal was
26. One from a bear is long and sharp.
27. Thomas broke his

When Legends Die Crossword 1 Answer Key

Across
2. Pierce flesh with a sharp object
4. Bessie bought Thomas a red one.
7. Tom had to learn to do it again.
8. Albert ___ Hand
9. Black ___
11. Footwear used to urge on horses
13. Baby bear
15. Deer family members
17. Thomas was from this Indian tribe.
18. Food from animals
19. Bucks and does
21. Cowboy's night stop
23. Bet on Tom
25. Killer Tom; Bear's Brother
27. Thomas's roommate
28. ___ Elk
29. Store owner
30. Mr. Left Hand

Down
1. He tended his beans and peppers.
3. Meo grew them
4. Metal object in a horse's mouth
5. Flogged Thomas for fighting
6. Thomas ___ Bull
9. Bear's Brother's mother
10. When the ___ Die
12. English teacher
14. Bear's ___ (Thomas)
16. Bessie bought one for Thomas.
18. Nurse Redmond
20. Luther and Thomas shared one.
21. Cowboy's leg protectors
22. Papers granting permission
24. Jim owned one
25. Path; place where animal was
26. One from a bear is long and sharp.
27. Thomas broke his

When Legends Die Crossword 2

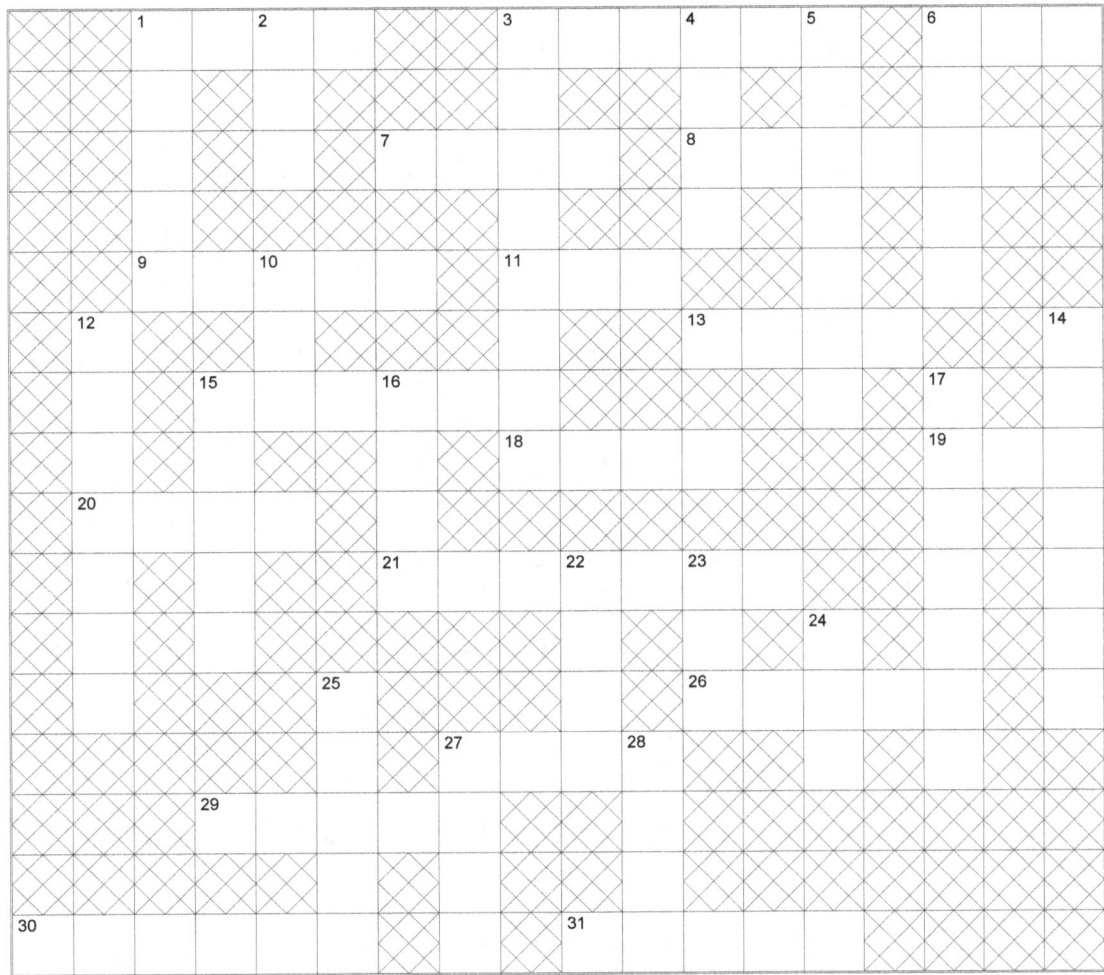

Across
1. Cowboy's night stop
3. Killer Tom; Bear's Brother
6. Metal object in a horse's mouth
7. One from a bear is long and sharp.
8. English teacher
9. Footwear used to urge on horses
11. Baby bear
13. Tom had to learn to do it again.
15. Bear's Brother's mother
18. Luther and Thomas shared one.
19. Bet on Tom
20. Food from animals
21. Bessie bought Thomas a red one.
26. Bessie bought one for Thomas.
27. Black ___
29. Path; place where animal was
30. Bows shoot them
31. Jim owned one

Down
1. Cowboy's leg protectors
2. He tended his beans and peppers.
3. Jim's last name
4. Nurse Redmond
5. Some Indians were stuck working there.
6. Carpentry teacher
10. Thomas was from this Indian tribe.
12. Papers granting permission
14. Nurse Mary
15. Thomas ___ Bull
16. Pierce flesh with a sharp object
17. Bear's ___ (Thomas)
22. Flogged Thomas for fighting
23. Deer family members
24. Store owner
25. Meo grew them
27. ___ Elk
28. Albert ___ Hand

When Legends Die Crossword 2 Answer Key

		1 C	A	2 M	P			3 T	H	4 O	M	5 A	S		6 B	I	T
		H		E				H		A		A			E		
		A		O		7 C	L	A	W		8 R	O	W	E	N	A	
		P				T				Y		M			N		
		9 S	P	10 U	R	S		11 C	U	B			I		Y		
	12 P			T				H			13 W	A	L	K			14 R
	E		15 B	E	S	16 S	I	E					L		17 B		E
	R		L			T		18 R	O	O	M				19 R	E	D
20 M	E	A	T			A									O		M
	I		C			21 B	L	22 A	N	23 K	E	T			T		O
	T		K					E		L			24 J		H		N
	S			25 B				I		26 K	N	I	F	E			D
				E			27 B	U	28 L	L			M		R		
			29 T	R	A	I	L		E								
				N			U		F								
30 A	R	R	O	W	S		E		31 S	T	O	R	E				

Across
1. Cowboy's night stop
3. Killer Tom; Bear's Brother
6. Metal object in a horse's mouth
7. One from a bear is long and sharp.
8. English teacher
9. Footwear used to urge on horses
11. Baby bear
13. Tom had to learn to do it again.
15. Bear's Brother's mother
18. Luther and Thomas shared one.
19. Bet on Tom
20. Food from animals
21. Bessie bought Thomas a red one.
26. Bessie bought one for Thomas.
27. Black ___
29. Path; place where animal was
30. Bows shoot them
31. Jim owned one

Down
1. Cowboy's leg protectors
2. He tended his beans and peppers.
3. Jim's last name
4. Nurse Redmond
5. Some Indians were stuck working there.
6. Carpentry teacher
10. Thomas was from this Indian tribe.
12. Papers granting permission
14. Nurse Mary
15. Thomas ___ Bull
16. Pierce flesh with a sharp object
17. Bear's ___ (Thomas)
22. Flogged Thomas for fighting
23. Deer family members
24. Store owner
25. Meo grew them
27. ___ Elk
28. Albert ___ Hand

When Legends Die Crossword 3

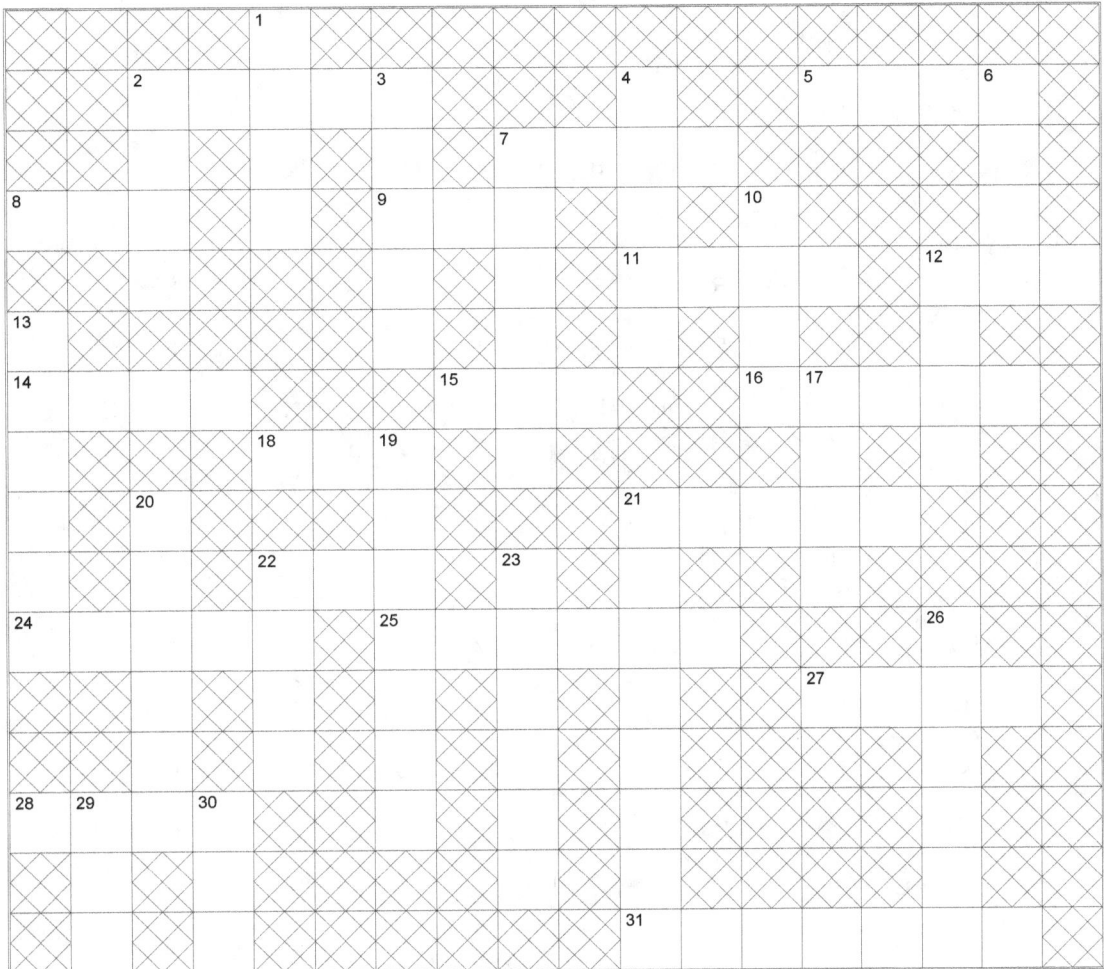

Across
2. Cowboy's leg protectors
5. Pierce flesh with a sharp object
7. Black ___
8. Store owner
9. Thomas was from this Indian tribe.
11. One from a bear is long and sharp.
12. Thomas broke his
14. Luther and Thomas shared one.
15. Metal object in a horse's mouth
16. Bessie bought one for Thomas.
18. Baby bear
21. Path; place where animal was
22. He tended his beans and peppers.
24. Jim owned one
25. Killer Tom; Bear's Brother
27. Water falling from the sky
28. Bucks and does
31. Nurse Mary

Down
1. Nurse Redmond
2. Cowboy's night stop
3. Footwear used to urge on horses
4. Thomas ___ Bull
6. ___ Elk
7. Bear's Brother's mother
10. Tom had to learn to do it again.
12. Albert ___ Hand
13. Bows shoot them
17. Flogged Thomas for fighting
19. Bear's ___ (Thomas)
20. He killed Frank No Deer.
21. Jim's last name
22. Food from animals
23. English teacher
26. Red's last name
29. Deer family members
30. Bet on Tom

When Legends Die Crossword 3 Answer Key

				1 M							
	2 C	H	3 A	P	S		4 B		5 S	T	A	6 B
	A		R		P	7 B	U	L	L			L
8 J	I	M		9 Y	U	T	E		A	10 W		U
	P				R		S		11 C	L	A	W	12 L	E	G
13 A					S		S		K		L		E
14 R	O	O	M			15 B	I	T		16 K	17 N	I	F	E
R			18 C	U	19 B	E				E		T
O		20 G		R			21 T	R	A	I	L
W		E		22 M	E	O	23 R		H		L
24 S	T	O	R	E		25 T	H	O	M	A	S		26 D
		R		A		H		W		T		27 R	A	I	N
		G		T		E		E		C			L
28 D	29 E	30 R				R		N		H			L
	L		E					A		E			O
	K		D				31 R	E	D	M	O	N	D

Across
2. Cowboy's leg protectors
5. Pierce flesh with a sharp object
7. Black ___
8. Store owner
9. Thomas was from this Indian tribe.
11. One from a bear is long and sharp.
12. Thomas broke his
14. Luther and Thomas shared one.
15. Metal object in a horse's mouth
16. Bessie bought one for Thomas.
18. Baby bear
21. Path; place where animal was
22. He tended his beans and peppers.
24. Jim owned one
25. Killer Tom; Bear's Brother
27. Water falling from the sky
28. Bucks and does
31. Nurse Mary

Down
1. Nurse Redmond
2. Cowboy's night stop
3. Footwear used to urge on horses
4. Thomas ___ Bull
6. ___ Elk
7. Bear's Brother's mother
10. Tom had to learn to do it again.
12. Albert ___ Hand
13. Bows shoot them
17. Flogged Thomas for fighting
19. Bear's ___ (Thomas)
20. He killed Frank No Deer.
21. Jim's last name
22. Food from animals
23. English teacher
26. Red's last name
29. Deer family members
30. Bet on Tom

When Legends Die Crossword 4

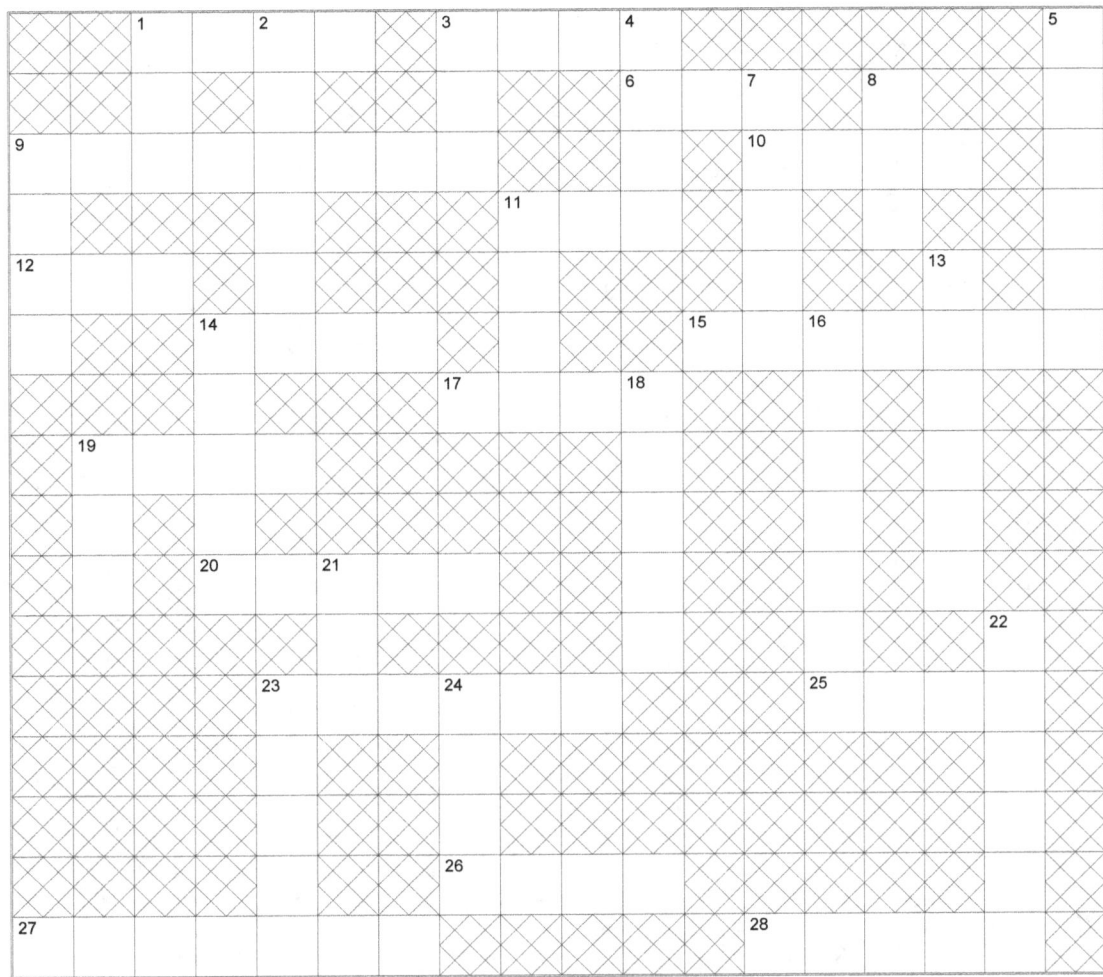

Across
1. Nurse Redmond
3. Luther and Thomas shared one.
6. Deer family members
9. Tom worked for him after the accident.
10. Flogged Thomas for fighting
11. Metal object in a horse's mouth
12. Thomas broke his
14. Cowboy's night stop
15. Papers granting permission
17. Albert ___ Hand
19. One from a bear is long and sharp.
20. Footwear used to urge on horses
23. Bear's Brother's mother
25. Bucks and does
26. Black ___
27. Bessie bought Thomas a red one.
28. Meo grew them

Down
1. He tended his beans and peppers.
2. English teacher
3. Bet on Tom
4. Food from animals
5. Killer Tom; Bear's Brother
7. Bessie bought one for Thomas.
8. Store owner
9. Tom had to learn to do it again.
11. ___ Elk
13. Red's last name
14. Cowboy's leg protectors
16. Nurse Mary
18. Path; place where animal was
19. Baby bear
21. Thomas was from this Indian tribe.
22. Bows shoot them
23. Thomas ___ Bull
24. Pierce flesh with a sharp object

When Legends Die Crossword 4 Answer Key

	1 M	2 A	R	Y		3 R	O	O	4 M			5 T
		E		O			E		6 E	7 L	8 K	J	H
9 W	O	O	D	W	A	R	D		A		10 N	E	I	L	O
A				E			11 B	I	T		I		M		M
12 L	E	G		N			L				F		13 D		A
K		14 C	A	M	P		U		15 P	16 E	R	M	I	T	S
		H			17 L	E	F	18 T		E		L	
19 C	L	A	W				R		D		L	
U		P					A		M		O	
B		20 S	21 P	U	R	S		I		O		N	
		T				L		N		22 A
	23 B	E	S	24 S	I	E		25 D	E	E	R
	L		T					R
	A		A					O
	C		26 B	U	L	L		W
27 B	L	A	N	K	E	T		28 B	E	A	N	S

Across
1. Nurse Redmond
3. Luther and Thomas shared one.
6. Deer family members
9. Tom worked for him after the accident.
10. Flogged Thomas for fighting
11. Metal object in a horse's mouth
12. Thomas broke his
14. Cowboy's night stop
15. Papers granting permission
17. Albert ___ Hand
19. One from a bear is long and sharp.
20. Footwear used to urge on horses
23. Bear's Brother's mother
25. Bucks and does
26. Black ___
27. Bessie bought Thomas a red one.
28. Meo grew them

Down
1. He tended his beans and peppers.
2. English teacher
3. Bet on Tom
4. Food from animals
5. Killer Tom; Bear's Brother
7. Bessie bought one for Thomas.
8. Store owner
9. Tom had to learn to do it again.
11. ___ Elk
13. Red's last name
14. Cowboy's leg protectors
16. Nurse Mary
18. Path; place where animal was
19. Baby bear
21. Thomas was from this Indian tribe.
22. Bows shoot them
23. Thomas ___ Bull
24. Pierce flesh with a sharp object

When Legends Die

WOODWARD	SPURS	WALK	CUB	PERMITS
BEAVERFOOT	BIT	DEER	STORE	MARY
BLANKET	TRAIL	FREE SPACE	BULL	ROOM
ARROWS	BLUE	RESERVATION	BENNY	NEIL
REDMOND	GEORGE	LEGENDS	ELK	RHYTHM

When Legends Die

CLAW	UTE	JIM	BLACK	LEG
RED	BEANS	THATCHER	STAB	BORLAND
CAMP	RAIN	FREE SPACE	DILLON	MEO
LUTHER	THOMAS	LEFT	CHAPS	ROWENA
BESSIE	MEAT	GRAYBACK	ALBERT	SAWMILL

When Legends Die

RED	TRAIL	THATCHER	BIT	BORLAND
STAB	REDMOND	BLACK	BEANS	ALBERT
AVALANCHE	GRAYBACK	FREE SPACE	ARROWS	JIM
SPURS	CHAPS	RHYTHM	DILLON	MEO
PERMITS	RESERVATION	CAMP	STORE	NEIL

When Legends Die

WOODWARD	ROOM	BEAVERFOOT	RAIN	CUB
BLUE	LEGENDS	ELK	THOMAS	BLANKET
GEORGE	UTE	FREE SPACE	BESSIE	BROTHER
LEG	MARY	ROWENA	SAWMILL	DEER
LUTHER	BENNY	BULL	KNIFE	CLAW

When Legends Die

GEORGE	REDMOND	WALK	ARROWS	RAIN
MEAT	LEG	STAB	CUB	JIM
LEGENDS	CLAW	FREE SPACE	THATCHER	BESSIE
GRAYBACK	SPURS	RED	LUTHER	BEANS
ROOM	WOODWARD	BLACK	BLANKET	BENNY

When Legends Die

NEIL	AVALANCHE	MARY	CHAPS	THOMAS
BLUE	UTE	DILLON	DEER	BROTHER
RHYTHM	ELK	FREE SPACE	ROWENA	KNIFE
BIT	RESERVATION	MEO	ALBERT	PERMITS
BORLAND	BEAVERFOOT	LEFT	STORE	SAWMILL

When Legends Die

GEORGE	SPURS	AVALANCHE	ALBERT	WOODWARD
RESERVATION	MEO	THATCHER	BIT	TRAIL
DILLON	ELK	FREE SPACE	NEIL	BLUE
WALK	BROTHER	PERMITS	DEER	KNIFE
ROOM	BLANKET	LUTHER	MARY	BLACK

When Legends Die

BESSIE	UTE	RED	RHYTHM	CUB
SAWMILL	RAIN	STORE	GRAYBACK	MEAT
BEAVERFOOT	BULL	FREE SPACE	BORLAND	STAB
CHAPS	JIM	LEG	REDMOND	THOMAS
ARROWS	CAMP	BENNY	LEGENDS	CLAW

When Legends Die

SPURS	BEANS	PERMITS	AVALANCHE	BEAVERFOOT
JIM	ARROWS	CUB	CLAW	BLACK
RESERVATION	MEO	FREE SPACE	LEG	UTE
BORLAND	RAIN	BROTHER	CAMP	MEAT
BLANKET	SAWMILL	ROWENA	THATCHER	GRAYBACK

When Legends Die

MARY	BLUE	BIT	RHYTHM	BESSIE
TRAIL	RED	BULL	DILLON	BENNY
REDMOND	NEIL	FREE SPACE	GEORGE	KNIFE
LEFT	WALK	STORE	ALBERT	THOMAS
DEER	ROOM	WOODWARD	CHAPS	ELK

When Legends Die

RAIN	THOMAS	BIT	SPURS	JIM
CLAW	MEAT	CAMP	LEFT	STAB
LEG	BLUE	FREE SPACE	CUB	BENNY
BEAVERFOOT	SAWMILL	BEANS	LUTHER	NEIL
ELK	LEGENDS	BLANKET	CHAPS	ARROWS

When Legends Die

BROTHER	BORLAND	BESSIE	MARY	DILLON
PERMITS	KNIFE	RESERVATION	UTE	GRAYBACK
MEO	WALK	FREE SPACE	WOODWARD	ALBERT
BULL	BLACK	STORE	AVALANCHE	REDMOND
DEER	GEORGE	TRAIL	THATCHER	RHYTHM

When Legends Die

BEAVERFOOT	ELK	WALK	BLACK	ARROWS
STAB	MARY	ROWENA	CUB	STORE
THATCHER	RAIN	FREE SPACE	BESSIE	ROOM
GEORGE	CHAPS	TRAIL	LUTHER	SAWMILL
LEGENDS	BLANKET	BIT	RESERVATION	MEAT

When Legends Die

SPURS	CAMP	DILLON	BULL	BROTHER
RED	MEO	DEER	JIM	LEG
BORLAND	UTE	FREE SPACE	LEFT	AVALANCHE
BLUE	BENNY	WOODWARD	BEANS	ALBERT
RHYTHM	KNIFE	THOMAS	GRAYBACK	REDMOND

When Legends Die

BLANKET	LEFT	BIT	BLUE	STAB
NEIL	LEG	ALBERT	GEORGE	WALK
BLACK	LEGENDS	FREE SPACE	RHYTHM	RESERVATION
CAMP	DILLON	THOMAS	BORLAND	BEANS
ARROWS	DEER	TRAIL	BENNY	BROTHER

When Legends Die

CHAPS	SAWMILL	BULL	MEO	MARY
GRAYBACK	STORE	KNIFE	RAIN	SPURS
AVALANCHE	RED	FREE SPACE	ROWENA	JIM
UTE	BEAVERFOOT	ELK	CLAW	THATCHER
WOODWARD	MEAT	CUB	REDMOND	ROOM

When Legends Die

STAB	LUTHER	DEER	MEO	AVALANCHE
WALK	CUB	BLANKET	LEGENDS	BLACK
TRAIL	KNIFE	FREE SPACE	STORE	ROWENA
NEIL	ELK	RED	BULL	DILLON
LEFT	REDMOND	RESERVATION	MEAT	MARY

When Legends Die

CLAW	CHAPS	RAIN	SAWMILL	BLUE
BEAVERFOOT	THATCHER	PERMITS	CAMP	JIM
GEORGE	LEG	FREE SPACE	WOODWARD	ARROWS
BROTHER	GRAYBACK	SPURS	THOMAS	ALBERT
BIT	ROOM	UTE	BESSIE	RHYTHM

When Legends Die

BROTHER	THATCHER	DEER	ROWENA	LEG
TRAIL	BIT	CLAW	BORLAND	ROOM
GRAYBACK	REDMOND	FREE SPACE	WALK	STORE
SAWMILL	RAIN	LEFT	KNIFE	ARROWS
PERMITS	RESERVATION	BLACK	BENNY	MEAT

When Legends Die

RED	LUTHER	BLUE	MARY	LEGENDS
AVALANCHE	BULL	MEO	UTE	BESSIE
BEAVERFOOT	BEANS	FREE SPACE	STAB	CAMP
ELK	JIM	NEIL	BLANKET	WOODWARD
CHAPS	THOMAS	GEORGE	DILLON	CUB

When Legends Die

BEAVERFOOT	AVALANCHE	GRAYBACK	LEGENDS	ELK
CAMP	NEIL	BLANKET	CUB	GEORGE
BIT	BULL	FREE SPACE	MEO	BROTHER
CHAPS	BEANS	WALK	STAB	STORE
CLAW	RAIN	BORLAND	ROOM	BLUE

When Legends Die

LEG	DEER	LEFT	MEAT	SAWMILL
TRAIL	JIM	KNIFE	MARY	WOODWARD
ARROWS	UTE	FREE SPACE	THATCHER	THOMAS
ROWENA	RED	DILLON	BESSIE	ALBERT
LUTHER	BENNY	REDMOND	PERMITS	RESERVATION

When Legends Die

RESERVATION	ELK	GEORGE	BORLAND	BLANKET
BLUE	STORE	ARROWS	LUTHER	ROWENA
TRAIL	BIT	FREE SPACE	SPURS	RAIN
BROTHER	LEGENDS	ALBERT	KNIFE	PERMITS
ROOM	NEIL	RED	REDMOND	LEG

When Legends Die

AVALANCHE	DEER	MEO	BENNY	MARY
BESSIE	THATCHER	BULL	GRAYBACK	LEFT
BEANS	WALK	FREE SPACE	THOMAS	MEAT
JIM	BLACK	DILLON	BEAVERFOOT	UTE
CHAPS	CLAW	WOODWARD	SAWMILL	CAMP

When Legends Die

BLANKET	NEIL	MARY	SAWMILL	BEAVERFOOT
CLAW	BORLAND	ROWENA	BLUE	LUTHER
STAB	STORE	FREE SPACE	BENNY	CHAPS
RESERVATION	TRAIL	KNIFE	BLACK	JIM
ALBERT	THATCHER	DILLON	PERMITS	AVALANCHE

When Legends Die

LEFT	LEGENDS	RHYTHM	LEG	WOODWARD
MEAT	REDMOND	CUB	BULL	WALK
ARROWS	BESSIE	FREE SPACE	GEORGE	RED
ROOM	GRAYBACK	BIT	BROTHER	UTE
RAIN	SPURS	BEANS	ELK	MEO

When Legends Die

ROOM	KNIFE	BEANS	ELK	DEER
REDMOND	THATCHER	CAMP	RED	ARROWS
RHYTHM	BEAVERFOOT	FREE SPACE	RESERVATION	BULL
BLANKET	RAIN	THOMAS	STORE	ALBERT
CLAW	NEIL	BLACK	MEO	BROTHER

When Legends Die

SPURS	LEGENDS	PERMITS	DILLON	GRAYBACK
LUTHER	WOODWARD	JIM	MARY	LEFT
BORLAND	STAB	FREE SPACE	MEAT	ROWENA
AVALANCHE	BLUE	TRAIL	LEG	BESSIE
UTE	CUB	SAWMILL	GEORGE	BENNY

When Legends Die

RAIN	ARROWS	NEIL	WALK	ROWENA
LUTHER	LEGENDS	STORE	UTE	BENNY
SAWMILL	RED	FREE SPACE	ROOM	REDMOND
BIT	MEO	BORLAND	ELK	KNIFE
GRAYBACK	AVALANCHE	BLACK	JIM	CUB

When Legends Die

MARY	CAMP	CHAPS	PERMITS	BEAVERFOOT
RHYTHM	TRAIL	BROTHER	THOMAS	BESSIE
BLANKET	SPURS	FREE SPACE	BLUE	MEAT
CLAW	LEFT	DEER	BEANS	ALBERT
THATCHER	GEORGE	RESERVATION	DILLON	LEG

When Legends Die

PERMITS	CLAW	ROOM	BULL	ROWENA
CHAPS	STORE	AVALANCHE	MARY	RED
BIT	DILLON	FREE SPACE	RHYTHM	BEANS
BLUE	BLANKET	LUTHER	LEFT	MEO
TRAIL	GRAYBACK	SPURS	RAIN	GEORGE

When Legends Die

WALK	BROTHER	SAWMILL	RESERVATION	STAB
BENNY	BORLAND	ARROWS	KNIFE	THATCHER
REDMOND	MEAT	FREE SPACE	ELK	BESSIE
JIM	BEAVERFOOT	WOODWARD	NEIL	LEGENDS
ALBERT	LEG	THOMAS	CUB	BLACK

When Legends Die Vocabulary Word List

No.	Word	Clue/Definition
1.	ABASHED	Ashamed; embarrassed
2.	ACCLIMATED	Became used to a condition
3.	ACRID	Harsh to the taste or smell
4.	AMBIGUOUS	Indefinite; open to several interpretations
5.	BAFFLED	Puzzled; perplexed; confused
6.	BECKONED	Summoned by using gestures
7.	CACHE	Hole where things can be hidden
8.	CONNIVING	Conspiring; plotting; pretending ignorance of a wrong
9.	CUFFED	Slapped
10.	DEFT	Skillful
11.	DEPRECIATING	Belittling; making less of something
12.	DERISION	Ridicule; scoffing; mocking
13.	DISCONSOLATE	Gloomy; hopelessly sad
14.	DUBIOUS	Doubtful
15.	EQUILIBRIUM	Balance
16.	EXPECTANCY	The state or act of looking forward to something
17.	FATHOM	Understand
18.	HAGGLED	Bargained; argued over terms
19.	INCONSEQUENTIALS	Things that don't matter or don't have significance
20.	INEVITABILITY	Quality of not being able to be avoided
21.	INFURIATED	Made very angry
22.	LEACHED	Removed soluble parts by running through a substance
23.	LEVERED	Pushed as if using a lever
24.	MALEVOLENT	Malicious; evil; wishing harm to others
25.	MORBIDLY	In a manner preoccupied by unwholesome matters
26.	ORNATELY	Elaborately
27.	PENANCE	An act done to show repentance for a wrong doing
28.	PERSISTENT	Refusing to give up or let go
29.	PINIONED	Restrained by restricting one's arms
30.	PLIANT	Bendable
31.	PLUME	A feather-like form, structure, or object
32.	PROVOCATIVE	Tending to provoke; exciting; stimulating
33.	RANCID	Rotten
34.	REMNANT	Something left over
35.	SATED	Completely filled or satisfied
36.	SINEW	Tendons
37.	SOLICITOUS	Attentive; full of desire; eager
38.	STIFLE	Hold back; suppress; repress
39.	SULLEN	Sulky; moody
40.	TACITURN	Not talkative
41.	TAUNTED	Teased
42.	WEARY	Tired
43.	ZEAL	Enthusiasm

When Legends Die Vocabulary Fill In The Blanks 1

_____ 1. Quality of not being able to be avoided
_____ 2. Harsh to the taste or smell
_____ 3. The state or act of looking forward to something
_____ 4. Hole where things can be hidden
_____ 5. Sulky; moody
_____ 6. Summoned by using gestures
_____ 7. Something left over
_____ 8. Hold back; suppress; repress
_____ 9. Gloomy; hopelessly sad
_____ 10. Rotten
_____ 11. Things that don't matter or don't have significance
_____ 12. Attentive; full of desire; eager
_____ 13. Indefinite; open to several interpretations
_____ 14. Removed soluble parts by running through a substance
_____ 15. Restrained by restricting one's arms
_____ 16. Ridicule; scoffing; mocking
_____ 17. Elaborately
_____ 18. Became used to a condition
_____ 19. Pushed as if using a lever
_____ 20. Enthusiasm

When Legends Die Vocabulary Fill In The Blanks 1 Answer Key

INEVITABILITY	1. Quality of not being able to be avoided
ACRID	2. Harsh to the taste or smell
EXPECTANCY	3. The state or act of looking forward to something
CACHE	4. Hole where things can be hidden
SULLEN	5. Sulky; moody
BECKONED	6. Summoned by using gestures
REMNANT	7. Something left over
STIFLE	8. Hold back; suppress; repress
DISCONSOLATE	9. Gloomy; hopelessly sad
RANCID	10. Rotten
INCONSEQUENTIALS	11. Things that don't matter or don't have significance
SOLICITOUS	12. Attentive; full of desire; eager
AMBIGUOUS	13. Indefinite; open to several interpretations
LEACHED	14. Removed soluble parts by running through a substance
PINIONED	15. Restrained by restricting one's arms
DERISION	16. Ridicule; scoffing; mocking
ORNATELY	17. Elaborately
ACCLIMATED	18. Became used to a condition
LEVERED	19. Pushed as if using a lever
ZEAL	20. Enthusiasm

When Legends Die Vocabulary Fill In The Blanks 2

_____ 1. Understand

_____ 2. Bendable

_____ 3. A feather-like form, structure, or object

_____ 4. Indefinite; open to several interpretations

_____ 5. Summoned by using gestures

_____ 6. Hole where things can be hidden

_____ 7. Quality of not being able to be avoided

_____ 8. Balance

_____ 9. An act done to show repentance for a wrong doing

_____ 10. Attentive; full of desire; eager

_____ 11. Pushed as if using a lever

_____ 12. Hold back; suppress; repress

_____ 13. Tending to provoke; exciting; stimulating

_____ 14. Slapped

_____ 15. Tendons

_____ 16. Not talkative

_____ 17. Ridicule; scoffing; mocking

_____ 18. Completely filled or satisfied

_____ 19. Skillful

_____ 20. Doubtful

When Legends Die Vocabulary Fill In The Blanks 2 Answer Key

FATHOM	1. Understand
PLIANT	2. Bendable
PLUME	3. A feather-like form, structure, or object
AMBIGUOUS	4. Indefinite; open to several interpretations
BECKONED	5. Summoned by using gestures
CACHE	6. Hole where things can be hidden
INEVITABILITY	7. Quality of not being able to be avoided
EQUILIBRIUM	8. Balance
PENANCE	9. An act done to show repentance for a wrong doing
SOLICITOUS	10. Attentive; full of desire; eager
LEVERED	11. Pushed as if using a lever
STIFLE	12. Hold back; suppress; repress
PROVOCATIVE	13. Tending to provoke; exciting; stimulating
CUFFED	14. Slapped
SINEW	15. Tendons
TACITURN	16. Not talkative
DERISION	17. Ridicule; scoffing; mocking
SATED	18. Completely filled or satisfied
DEFT	19. Skillful
DUBIOUS	20. Doubtful

When Legends Die Vocabulary Fill In The Blanks 3

_____ 1. Indefinite; open to several interpretations

_____ 2. Restrained by restricting one's arms

_____ 3. Puzzled; perplexed; confused

_____ 4. Something left over

_____ 5. Gloomy; hopelessly sad

_____ 6. Refusing to give up or let go

_____ 7. Understand

_____ 8. Malicious; evil; wishing harm to others

_____ 9. Tired

_____ 10. Hold back; suppress; repress

_____ 11. Hole where things can be hidden

_____ 12. Tendons

_____ 13. Elaborately

_____ 14. Attentive; full of desire; eager

_____ 15. Rotten

_____ 16. Completely filled or satisfied

_____ 17. Balance

_____ 18. Summoned by using gestures

_____ 19. Doubtful

_____ 20. Ridicule; scoffing; mocking

When Legends Die Vocabulary Fill In The Blanks 3 Answer Key

AMBIGUOUS	1. Indefinite; open to several interpretations
PINIONED	2. Restrained by restricting one's arms
BAFFLED	3. Puzzled; perplexed; confused
REMNANT	4. Something left over
DISCONSOLATE	5. Gloomy; hopelessly sad
PERSISTENT	6. Refusing to give up or let go
FATHOM	7. Understand
MALEVOLENT	8. Malicious; evil; wishing harm to others
WEARY	9. Tired
STIFLE	10. Hold back; suppress; repress
CACHE	11. Hole where things can be hidden
SINEW	12. Tendons
ORNATELY	13. Elaborately
SOLICITOUS	14. Attentive; full of desire; eager
RANCID	15. Rotten
SATED	16. Completely filled or satisfied
EQUILIBRIUM	17. Balance
BECKONED	18. Summoned by using gestures
DUBIOUS	19. Doubtful
DERISION	20. Ridicule; scoffing; mocking

When Legends Die Vocabulary Fill In The Blanks 4

_____ 1. Completely filled or satisfied
_____ 2. Bendable
_____ 3. Removed soluble parts by running through a substance
_____ 4. The state or act of looking forward to something
_____ 5. An act done to show repentance for a wrong doing
_____ 6. Puzzled; perplexed; confused
_____ 7. Conspiring; plotting; pretending ignorance of a wrong
_____ 8. Ashamed; embarrassed
_____ 9. Belittling; making less of something
_____ 10. Summoned by using gestures
_____ 11. Understand
_____ 12. Not talkative
_____ 13. Balance
_____ 14. Hold back; suppress; repress
_____ 15. Rotten
_____ 16. Something left over
_____ 17. Refusing to give up or let go
_____ 18. Pushed as if using a lever
_____ 19. Harsh to the taste or smell
_____ 20. In a manner preoccupied by unwholesome matters

When Legends Die Vocabulary Fill In The Blanks 4 Answer Key

SATED	1. Completely filled or satisfied
PLIANT	2. Bendable
LEACHED	3. Removed soluble parts by running through a substance
EXPECTANCY	4. The state or act of looking forward to something
PENANCE	5. An act done to show repentance for a wrong doing
BAFFLED	6. Puzzled; perplexed; confused
CONNIVING	7. Conspiring; plotting; pretending ignorance of a wrong
ABASHED	8. Ashamed; embarrassed
DEPRECIATING	9. Belittling; making less of something
BECKONED	10. Summoned by using gestures
FATHOM	11. Understand
TACITURN	12. Not talkative
EQUILIBRIUM	13. Balance
STIFLE	14. Hold back; suppress; repress
RANCID	15. Rotten
REMNANT	16. Something left over
PERSISTENT	17. Refusing to give up or let go
LEVERED	18. Pushed as if using a lever
ACRID	19. Harsh to the taste or smell
MORBIDLY	20. In a manner preoccupied by unwholesome matters

When Legends Die Vocabulary Matching 1

___ 1. PERSISTENT   A. Enthusiasm
___ 2. ORNATELY   B. Summoned by using gestures
___ 3. CONNIVING   C. Malicious; evil; wishing harm to others
___ 4. EXPECTANCY   D. Tired
___ 5. DUBIOUS   E. Elaborately
___ 6. PENANCE   F. Harsh to the taste or smell
___ 7. FATHOM   G. Ashamed; embarrassed
___ 8. SOLICITOUS   H. Belittling; making less of something
___ 9. ABASHED   I. A feather-like form, structure, or object
___ 10. PROVOCATIVE   J. Sulky; moody
___ 11. BECKONED   K. Became used to a condition
___ 12. DEPRECIATING   L. Tendons
___ 13. ACRID   M. Gloomy; hopelessly sad
___ 14. DISCONSOLATE   N. Doubtful
___ 15. ACCLIMATED   O. Understand
___ 16. MALEVOLENT   P. Attentive; full of desire; eager
___ 17. HAGGLED   Q. Something left over
___ 18. ZEAL   R. Conspiring; plotting; pretending ignorance of a wrong
___ 19. PINIONED   S. Refusing to give up or let go
___ 20. SINEW   T. Bendable
___ 21. PLIANT   U. Tending to provoke; exciting; stimulating
___ 22. WEARY   V. The state or act of looking forward to something
___ 23. PLUME   W. Bargained; argued over terms
___ 24. REMNANT   X. An act done to show repentance for a wrong doing
___ 25. SULLEN   Y. Restrained by restricting one's arms

When Legends Die Vocabulary Matching 1 Answer Key

S - 1. PERSISTENT		A. Enthusiasm
E - 2. ORNATELY		B. Summoned by using gestures
R - 3. CONNIVING		C. Malicious; evil; wishing harm to others
V - 4. EXPECTANCY		D. Tired
N - 5. DUBIOUS		E. Elaborately
X - 6. PENANCE		F. Harsh to the taste or smell
O - 7. FATHOM		G. Ashamed; embarrassed
P - 8. SOLICITOUS		H. Belittling; making less of something
G - 9. ABASHED		I. A feather-like form, structure, or object
U - 10. PROVOCATIVE		J. Sulky; moody
B - 11. BECKONED		K. Became used to a condition
H - 12. DEPRECIATING		L. Tendons
F - 13. ACRID		M. Gloomy; hopelessly sad
M - 14. DISCONSOLATE		N. Doubtful
K - 15. ACCLIMATED		O. Understand
C - 16. MALEVOLENT		P. Attentive; full of desire; eager
W - 17. HAGGLED		Q. Something left over
A - 18. ZEAL		R. Conspiring; plotting; pretending ignorance of a wrong
Y - 19. PINIONED		S. Refusing to give up or let go
L - 20. SINEW		T. Bendable
T - 21. PLIANT		U. Tending to provoke; exciting; stimulating
D - 22. WEARY		V. The state or act of looking forward to something
I - 23. PLUME		W. Bargained; argued over terms
Q - 24. REMNANT		X. An act done to show repentance for a wrong doing
J - 25. SULLEN		Y. Restrained by restricting one's arms

When Legends Die Vocabulary Matching 2

___ 1. BAFFLED   A. Summoned by using gestures
___ 2. WEARY   B. An act done to show repentance for a wrong doing
___ 3. FATHOM   C. Pushed as if using a lever
___ 4. ORNATELY   D. Balance
___ 5. DISCONSOLATE   E. Made very angry
___ 6. PENANCE   F. Puzzled; perplexed; confused
___ 7. MALEVOLENT   G. Gloomy; hopelessly sad
___ 8. ACRID   H. Teased
___ 9. TAUNTED   I. Bendable
___10. BECKONED   J. Sulky; moody
___11. PROVOCATIVE   K. Hold back; suppress; repress
___12. SULLEN   L. Refusing to give up or let go
___13. LEVERED   M. Malicious; evil; wishing harm to others
___14. INEVITABILITY   N. Quality of not being able to be avoided
___15. EQUILIBRIUM   O. Tending to provoke; exciting; stimulating
___16. DEPRECIATING   P. Something left over
___17. STIFLE   Q. Belittling; making less of something
___18. SOLICITOUS   R. Things that don't matter or don't have significance
___19. TACITURN   S. Understand
___20. PLIANT   T. Tired
___21. PERSISTENT   U. Attentive; full of desire; eager
___22. PLUME   V. Elaborately
___23. REMNANT   W. A feather-like form, structure, or object
___24. INFURIATED   X. Not talkative
___25. INCONSEQUENTIALS Y. Harsh to the taste or smell

When Legends Die Vocabulary Matching 2 Answer Key

F - 1.	BAFFLED	A.	Summoned by using gestures
T - 2.	WEARY	B.	An act done to show repentance for a wrong doing
S - 3.	FATHOM	C.	Pushed as if using a lever
V - 4.	ORNATELY	D.	Balance
G - 5.	DISCONSOLATE	E.	Made very angry
B - 6.	PENANCE	F.	Puzzled; perplexed; confused
M - 7.	MALEVOLENT	G.	Gloomy; hopelessly sad
Y - 8.	ACRID	H.	Teased
H - 9.	TAUNTED	I.	Bendable
A - 10.	BECKONED	J.	Sulky; moody
O - 11.	PROVOCATIVE	K.	Hold back; suppress; repress
J - 12.	SULLEN	L.	Refusing to give up or let go
C - 13.	LEVERED	M.	Malicious; evil; wishing harm to others
N - 14.	INEVITABILITY	N.	Quality of not being able to be avoided
D - 15.	EQUILIBRIUM	O.	Tending to provoke; exciting; stimulating
Q - 16.	DEPRECIATING	P.	Something left over
K - 17.	STIFLE	Q.	Belittling; making less of something
U - 18.	SOLICITOUS	R.	Things that don't matter or don't have significance
X - 19.	TACITURN	S.	Understand
I - 20.	PLIANT	T.	Tired
L - 21.	PERSISTENT	U.	Attentive; full of desire; eager
W - 22.	PLUME	V.	Elaborately
P - 23.	REMNANT	W.	A feather-like form, structure, or object
E - 24.	INFURIATED	X.	Not talkative
R - 25.	INCONSEQUENTIALS	Y.	Harsh to the taste or smell

When Legends Die Vocabulary Matching 3

___ 1. MORBIDLY   A. The state or act of looking forward to something
___ 2. ZEAL   B. Sulky; moody
___ 3. ABASHED   C. Understand
___ 4. RANCID   D. Refusing to give up or let go
___ 5. AMBIGUOUS   E. Conspiring; plotting; pretending ignorance of a wrong
___ 6. STIFLE   F. Bargained; argued over terms
___ 7. CUFFED   G. Malicious; evil; wishing harm to others
___ 8. PLUME   H. Teased
___ 9. INEVITABILITY   I. Belittling; making less of something
___10. SULLEN   J. Puzzled; perplexed; confused
___11. CONNIVING   K. Became used to a condition
___12. DERISION   L. Bendable
___13. MALEVOLENT   M. Completely filled or satisfied
___14. SATED   N. Hold back; suppress; repress
___15. PERSISTENT   O. Ridicule; scoffing; mocking
___16. FATHOM   P. Rotten
___17. PLIANT   Q. Ashamed; embarrassed
___18. HAGGLED   R. Indefinite; open to several interpretations
___19. DEPRECIATING   S. Harsh to the taste or smell
___20. ACRID   T. In a manner preoccupied by unwholesome matters
___21. ACCLIMATED   U. Quality of not being able to be avoided
___22. EXPECTANCY   V. Slapped
___23. TAUNTED   W. An act done to show repentance for a wrong doing
___24. BAFFLED   X. A feather-like form, structure, or object
___25. PENANCE   Y. Enthusiasm

When Legends Die Vocabulary Matching 3 Answer Key

T - 1.	MORBIDLY	A. The state or act of looking forward to something
Y - 2.	ZEAL	B. Sulky; moody
Q - 3.	ABASHED	C. Understand
P - 4.	RANCID	D. Refusing to give up or let go
R - 5.	AMBIGUOUS	E. Conspiring; plotting; pretending ignorance of a wrong
N - 6.	STIFLE	F. Bargained; argued over terms
V - 7.	CUFFED	G. Malicious; evil; wishing harm to others
X - 8.	PLUME	H. Teased
U - 9.	INEVITABILITY	I. Belittling; making less of something
B - 10.	SULLEN	J. Puzzled; perplexed; confused
E - 11.	CONNIVING	K. Became used to a condition
O - 12.	DERISION	L. Bendable
G - 13.	MALEVOLENT	M. Completely filled or satisfied
M - 14.	SATED	N. Hold back; suppress; repress
D - 15.	PERSISTENT	O. Ridicule; scoffing; mocking
C - 16.	FATHOM	P. Rotten
L - 17.	PLIANT	Q. Ashamed; embarrassed
F - 18.	HAGGLED	R. Indefinite; open to several interpretations
I - 19.	DEPRECIATING	S. Harsh to the taste or smell
S - 20.	ACRID	T. In a manner preoccupied by unwholesome matters
K - 21.	ACCLIMATED	U. Quality of not being able to be avoided
A - 22.	EXPECTANCY	V. Slapped
H - 23.	TAUNTED	W. An act done to show repentance for a wrong doing
J - 24.	BAFFLED	X. A feather-like form, structure, or object
W - 25.	PENANCE	Y. Enthusiasm

When Legends Die Vocabulary Matching 4

___ 1. AMBIGUOUS   A. Something left over
___ 2. EQUILIBRIUM   B. Things that don't matter or don't have significance
___ 3. RANCID   C. Refusing to give up or let go
___ 4. INEVITABILITY   D. Quality of not being able to be avoided
___ 5. ACRID   E. Became used to a condition
___ 6. CUFFED   F. Indefinite; open to several interpretations
___ 7. INCONSEQUENTIALS   G. Attentive; full of desire; eager
___ 8. DUBIOUS   H. Slapped
___ 9. WEARY   I. Conspiring; plotting; pretending ignorance of a wrong
___10. LEACHED   J. Summoned by using gestures
___11. ACCLIMATED   K. Bendable
___12. PINIONED   L. Rotten
___13. REMNANT   M. Puzzled; perplexed; confused
___14. INFURIATED   N. Tendons
___15. CONNIVING   O. Removed soluble parts by running through a substance
___16. FATHOM   P. Tired
___17. BECKONED   Q. Teased
___18. SOLICITOUS   R. Harsh to the taste or smell
___19. ORNATELY   S. Completely filled or satisfied
___20. SINEW   T. Made very angry
___21. PLIANT   U. Restrained by restricting one's arms
___22. BAFFLED   V. Understand
___23. TAUNTED   W. Balance
___24. SATED   X. Elaborately
___25. PERSISTENT   Y. Doubtful

When Legends Die Vocabulary Matching 4 Answer Key

F - 1. AMBIGUOUS		A. Something left over
W - 2. EQUILIBRIUM		B. Things that don't matter or don't have significance
L - 3. RANCID		C. Refusing to give up or let go
D - 4. INEVITABILITY		D. Quality of not being able to be avoided
R - 5. ACRID		E. Became used to a condition
H - 6. CUFFED		F. Indefinite; open to several interpretations
B - 7. INCONSEQUENTIALS		G. Attentive; full of desire; eager
Y - 8. DUBIOUS		H. Slapped
P - 9. WEARY		I. Conspiring; plotting; pretending ignorance of a wrong
O - 10. LEACHED		J. Summoned by using gestures
E - 11. ACCLIMATED		K. Bendable
U - 12. PINIONED		L. Rotten
A - 13. REMNANT		M. Puzzled; perplexed; confused
T - 14. INFURIATED		N. Tendons
I - 15. CONNIVING		O. Removed soluble parts by running through a substance
V - 16. FATHOM		P. Tired
J - 17. BECKONED		Q. Teased
G - 18. SOLICITOUS		R. Harsh to the taste or smell
X - 19. ORNATELY		S. Completely filled or satisfied
N - 20. SINEW		T. Made very angry
K - 21. PLIANT		U. Restrained by restricting one's arms
M - 22. BAFFLED		V. Understand
Q - 23. TAUNTED		W. Balance
S - 24. SATED		X. Elaborately
C - 25. PERSISTENT		Y. Doubtful

When Legends Die Vocabulary Magic Squares 1

Match the definition with the vocabulary word. Put your answers in the magic squares below. When your answers are correct, all columns and rows will add to the same number.

A. STIFLE
B. ORNATELY
C. ACRID
D. AMBIGUOUS
E. WEARY
F. HAGGLED
G. BAFFLED
H. SINEW
I. CACHE
J. EXPECTANCY
K. CUFFED
L. LEVERED
M. RANCID
N. PENANCE
O. LEACHED
P. PROVOCATIVE

1. Tendons
2. Hold back; suppress; repress
3. Elaborately
4. Puzzled; perplexed; confused
5. The state or act of looking forward to something
6. Removed soluble parts by running through a substance
7. Tending to provoke; exciting; stimulating
8. Hole where things can be hidden
9. Slapped
10. An act done to show repentance for a wrong doing
11. Rotten
12. Pushed as if using a lever
13. Tired
14. Indefinite; open to several interpretations
15. Harsh to the taste or smell
16. Bargained; argued over terms

A=	B=	C=	D=
E=	F=	G=	H=
I=	J=	K=	L=
M=	N=	O=	P=

When Legends Die Vocabulary Magic Squares 1 Answer Key

Match the definition with the vocabulary word. Put your answers in the magic squares below. When your answers are correct, all columns and rows will add to the same number.

A. STIFLE
B. ORNATELY
C. ACRID
D. AMBIGUOUS
E. WEARY
F. HAGGLED
G. BAFFLED
H. SINEW
I. CACHE
J. EXPECTANCY
K. CUFFED
L. LEVERED
M. RANCID
N. PENANCE
O. LEACHED
P. PROVOCATIVE

1. Tendons
2. Hold back; suppress; repress
3. Elaborately
4. Puzzled; perplexed; confused
5. The state or act of looking forward to something
6. Removed soluble parts by running through a substance
7. Tending to provoke; exciting; stimulating
8. Hole where things can be hidden
9. Slapped
10. An act done to show repentance for a wrong doing
11. Rotten
12. Pushed as if using a lever
13. Tired
14. Indefinite; open to several interpretations
15. Harsh to the taste or smell
16. Bargained; argued over terms

A=2	B=3	C=15	D=14
E=13	F=16	G=4	H=1
I=8	J=5	K=9	L=12
M=11	N=10	O=6	P=7

When Legends Die Vocabulary Magic Squares 2

Match the definition with the vocabulary word. Put your answers in the magic squares below. When your answers are correct, all columns and rows will add to the same number.

A. BECKONED
B. INCONSEQUENTIALS
C. AMBIGUOUS
D. TACITURN
E. PLIANT
F. DERISION
G. LEACHED
H. PERSISTENT
I. STIFLE
J. ACRID
K. INFURIATED
L. PLUME
M. PINIONED
N. EXPECTANCY
O. TAUNTED
P. SOLICITOUS

1. Summoned by using gestures
2. The state or act of looking forward to something
3. Harsh to the taste or smell
4. Bendable
5. Removed soluble parts by running through a substance
6. A feather-like form, structure, or object
7. Attentive; full of desire; eager
8. Indefinite; open to several interpretations
9. Teased
10. Not talkative
11. Refusing to give up or let go
12. Made very angry
13. Hold back; suppress; repress
14. Ridicule; scoffing; mocking
15. Things that don't matter or don't have significance
16. Restrained by restricting one's arms

A=	B=	C=	D=
E=	F=	G=	H=
I=	J=	K=	L=
M=	N=	O=	P=

When Legends Die Vocabulary Magic Squares 2 Answer Key

Match the definition with the vocabulary word. Put your answers in the magic squares below. When your answers are correct, all columns and rows will add to the same number.

A. BECKONED
B. INCONSEQUENTIALS
C. AMBIGUOUS
D. TACITURN
E. PLIANT
F. DERISION
G. LEACHED
H. PERSISTENT
I. STIFLE
J. ACRID
K. INFURIATED
L. PLUME
M. PINIONED
N. EXPECTANCY
O. TAUNTED
P. SOLICITOUS

1. Summoned by using gestures
2. The state or act of looking forward to something
3. Harsh to the taste or smell
4. Bendable
5. Removed soluble parts by running through a substance
6. A feather-like form, structure, or object
7. Attentive; full of desire; eager
8. Indefinite; open to several interpretations
9. Teased
10. Not talkative
11. Refusing to give up or let go
12. Made very angry
13. Hold back; suppress; repress
14. Ridicule; scoffing; mocking
15. Things that don't matter or don't have significance
16. Restrained by restricting one's arms

A=1	B=15	C=8	D=10
E=4	F=14	G=5	H=11
I=13	J=3	K=12	L=6
M=16	N=2	O=9	P=7

When Legends Die Vocabulary Magic Squares 3

Match the definition with the vocabulary word. Put your answers in the magic squares below. When your answers are correct, all columns and rows will add to the same number.

A. EQUILIBRIUM
B. TAUNTED
C. LEACHED
D. SINEW
E. DUBIOUS
F. INEVITABILITY
G. CACHE
H. FATHOM
I. EXPECTANCY
J. CONNIVING
K. MALEVOLENT
L. AMBIGUOUS
M. MORBIDLY
N. PROVOCATIVE
O. STIFLE
P. PENANCE

1. Teased
2. Hole where things can be hidden
3. Malicious; evil; wishing harm to others
4. Tending to provoke; exciting; stimulating
5. In a manner preoccupied by unwholesome matters
6. Indefinite; open to several interpretations
7. Understand
8. Balance
9. An act done to show repentance for a wrong doing
10. The state or act of looking forward to something
11. Doubtful
12. Tendons
13. Removed soluble parts by running through a substance
14. Quality of not being able to be avoided
15. Conspiring; plotting; pretending ignorance of a wrong
16. Hold back; suppress; repress

A=	B=	C=	D=
E=	F=	G=	H=
I=	J=	K=	L=
M=	N=	O=	P=

When Legends Die Vocabulary Magic Squares 3 Answer Key

Match the definition with the vocabulary word. Put your answers in the magic squares below. When your answers are correct, all columns and rows will add to the same number.

A. EQUILIBRIUM
B. TAUNTED
C. LEACHED
D. SINEW
E. DUBIOUS
F. INEVITABILITY
G. CACHE
H. FATHOM
I. EXPECTANCY
J. CONNIVING
K. MALEVOLENT
L. AMBIGUOUS
M. MORBIDLY
N. PROVOCATIVE
O. STIFLE
P. PENANCE

1. Teased
2. Hole where things can be hidden
3. Malicious; evil; wishing harm to others
4. Tending to provoke; exciting; stimulating
5. In a manner preoccupied by unwholesome matters
6. Indefinite; open to several interpretations
7. Understand
8. Balance
9. An act done to show repentance for a wrong doing
10. The state or act of looking forward to something
11. Doubtful
12. Tendons
13. Removed soluble parts by running through a substance
14. Quality of not being able to be avoided
15. Conspiring; plotting; pretending ignorance of a wrong
16. Hold back; suppress; repress

A=8	B=1	C=13	D=12
E=11	F=14	G=2	H=7
I=10	J=15	K=3	L=6
M=5	N=4	O=16	P=9

When Legends Die Vocabulary Magic Squares 4

Match the definition with the vocabulary word. Put your answers in the magic squares below. When your answers are correct, all columns and rows will add to the same number.

A. LEACHED
B. CUFFED
C. DISCONSOLATE
D. HAGGLED
E. TAUNTED
F. INFURIATED
G. CACHE
H. SULLEN
I. SATED
J. WEARY
K. PINIONED
L. SOLICITOUS
M. ORNATELY
N. STIFLE
O. RANCID
P. MORBIDLY

1. Made very angry
2. Completely filled or satisfied
3. Rotten
4. Bargained; argued over terms
5. Elaborately
6. Slapped
7. Sulky; moody
8. Restrained by restricting one's arms
9. Gloomy; hopelessly sad
10. In a manner preoccupied by unwholesome matters
11. Tired
12. Teased
13. Attentive; full of desire; eager
14. Hole where things can be hidden
15. Removed soluble parts by running through a substance
16. Hold back; suppress; repress

A=	B=	C=	D=
E=	F=	G=	H=
I=	J=	K=	L=
M=	N=	O=	P=

When Legends Die Vocabulary Magic Squares 4 Answer Key

Match the definition with the vocabulary word. Put your answers in the magic squares below. When your answers are correct, all columns and rows will add to the same number.

A. LEACHED
B. CUFFED
C. DISCONSOLATE
D. HAGGLED
E. TAUNTED
F. INFURIATED
G. CACHE
H. SULLEN
I. SATED
J. WEARY
K. PINIONED
L. SOLICITOUS
M. ORNATELY
N. STIFLE
O. RANCID
P. MORBIDLY

1. Made very angry
2. Completely filled or satisfied
3. Rotten
4. Bargained; argued over terms
5. Elaborately
6. Slapped
7. Sulky; moody
8. Restrained by restricting one's arms
9. Gloomy; hopelessly sad
10. In a manner preoccupied by unwholesome matters
11. Tired
12. Teased
13. Attentive; full of desire; eager
14. Hole where things can be hidden
15. Removed soluble parts by running through a substance
16. Hold back; suppress; repress

A=15	B=6	C=9	D=4
E=12	F=1	G=14	H=7
I=2	J=11	K=8	L=13
M=5	N=16	O=3	P=10

When Legends Die Vocabulary Word Search 1

Words are placed backwards, forward, diagonally, up and down. Clues listed below can help you find the words. Circle the hidden vocabulary words in the maze.

```
W E A R Y T A U N T E D J V D I R C A Z
C H S L G G X W H W E W R E P Z D Q D
O C B E S X X A E N Z B T I T L E E D R
N A J A Z T G N O K L A E N A U A F Z K
N C D C B G I I T N M C D C S M L T W T
I U C H L S N F E I O P E O K E H H J P
V F J E T I Z L L S H E P N R O T T K L
I F D D P A L C U E T R R S A M N D N Y
N E L H S U C O B A A S E E N O A E P J
G D G E S A T I L V F I C Q C R N H D X
X L T V V I X O T P B S I U I B M S F F
P Z V T C E S L B U Y T A E D I E A F R
D D D I H N R P M D R E T N L D R B M Y
S U L D O Q N E H E K N I T M L X A C Y
Q O B C F J Z N D R T T N I P Y C N B D
S Q S I B Q S A J I W X G A J W A W A N
F I L Z O N X N M S P B W L J T W V F L
D Y S H F U R C V I G L L S C L D K F B
F P F D X S S E K O Q W I E Z J S Z L T
H M A L E V O L E N T M P A S W N C E V
P A M B I G U O U S H X Y P N W H B D V
I N F U R I A T E D E O R N A T E L Y X
```

A feather-like form, structure, or object (5)
An act done to show repentance for a wrong doing (7)
Ashamed; embarrassed (7)
Attentive; full of desire; eager (10)
Bargained; argued over terms (7)
Became used to a condition (10)
Belittling; making less of something (12)
Bendable (6)
Completely filled or satisfied (5)
Conspiring; plotting; pretending ignorance of a wrong (9)
Doubtful (7)
Elaborately (8)
Enthusiasm (4)
Gloomy; hopelessly sad (12)
Harsh to the taste or smell (5)
Hold back; suppress; repress (6)
Hole where things can be hidden (5)
In a manner preoccupied by unwholesome matters (8)
Indefinite; open to several interpretations (9)
Made very angry (10)

Malicious; evil; wishing harm to others (10)
Not talkative (8)
Pushed as if using a lever (7)
Puzzled; perplexed; confused (7)
Refusing to give up or let go (10)
Removed soluble parts by running through a substance (7)
Restrained by restricting one's arms (8)
Ridicule; scoffing; mocking (8)
Rotten (6)
Skillful (4)
Slapped (6)
Something left over (7)
Sulky; moody (6)
Summoned by using gestures (8)
Teased (7)
Tendons (5)
The state or act of looking forward to something (10)
Things that don't matter or don't have significance (16)
Tired (5)
Understand (6)

When Legends Die Vocabulary Word Search 1 Answer Key

Words are placed backwards, forward, diagonally, up and down. Clues listed below can help you find the words. Circle the hidden vocabulary words in the maze.

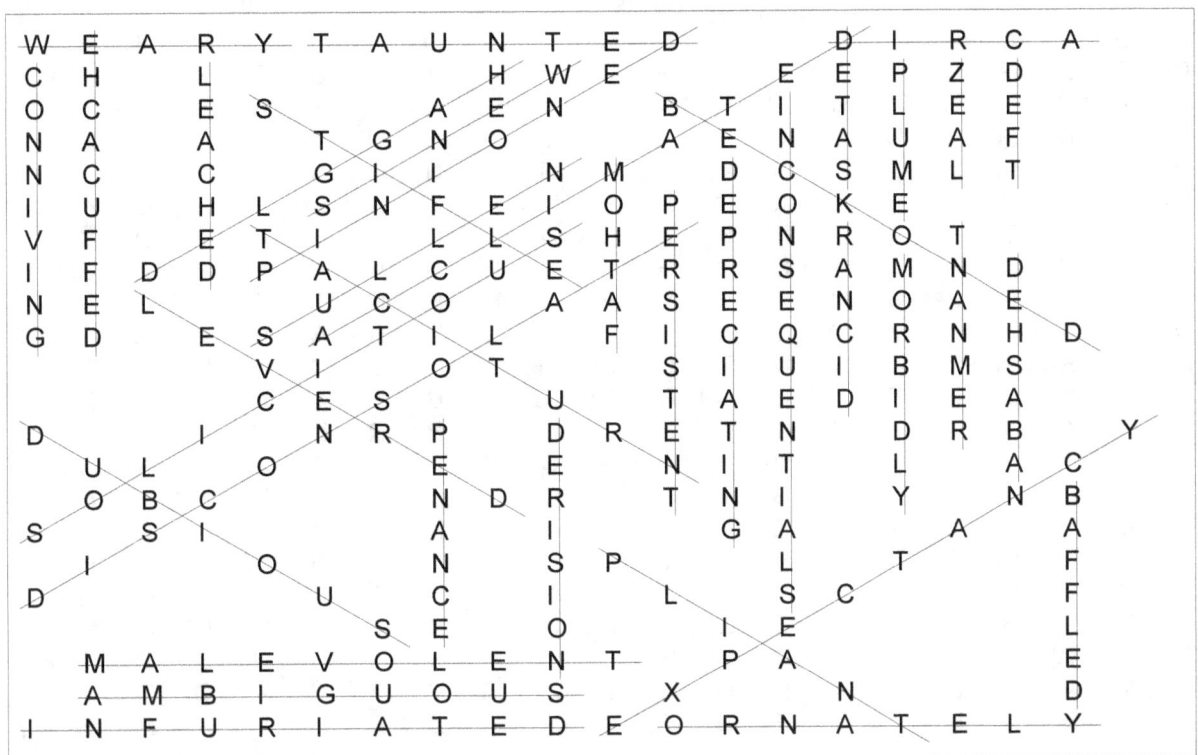

A feather-like form, structure, or object (5)
An act done to show repentance for a wrong doing (7)
Ashamed; embarrassed (7)
Attentive; full of desire; eager (10)
Bargained; argued over terms (7)
Became used to a condition (10)
Belittling; making less of something (12)
Bendable (6)
Completely filled or satisfied (5)
Conspiring; plotting; pretending ignorance of a wrong (9)
Doubtful (7)
Elaborately (8)
Enthusiasm (4)
Gloomy; hopelessly sad (12)
Harsh to the taste or smell (5)
Hold back; suppress; repress (6)
Hole where things can be hidden (5)
In a manner preoccupied by unwholesome matters (8)
Indefinite; open to several interpretations (9)
Made very angry (10)

Malicious; evil; wishing harm to others (10)
Not talkative (8)
Pushed as if using a lever (7)
Puzzled; perplexed; confused (7)
Refusing to give up or let go (10)
Removed soluble parts by running through a substance (7)
Restrained by restricting one's arms (8)
Ridicule; scoffing; mocking (8)
Rotten (6)
Skillful (4)
Slapped (6)
Something left over (7)
Sulky; moody (6)
Summoned by using gestures (8)
Teased (7)
Tendons (5)
The state or act of looking forward to something (10)
Things that don't matter or don't have significance (16)
Tired (5)
Understand (6)

When Legends Die Vocabulary Word Search 2

Words are placed backwards, forward, diagonally, up and down. Clues listed below can help you find the words. Circle the hidden vocabulary words in the maze.

```
T G B X D B S O L I C I T O U S L R H B
P S E G K J A D P E C F L B R S S E A F
Y T C P G F B F P K A O P Y A R U M G Q
P I K M D C B T F C T C N S N I L N G Z
N F O M E J C N W L F G H N C N L A L B
D L N B H H W A D F F R E E I E E N E K
Z E E T S U O I B U D D X Q D V N T D Y
P E D Z A K R L M E E E P U V I I E Z C
E V A S B C C P R T R T E I B T T N K M
N Q O L A V V E N M I A C L R A P I G G
A V R W G Z V U T O S M T I S B L N N T
N R N E M E A Q A R I I A B P I U F I F
C X A A L T W N C B O L N R R L M U T T
E Y T R C M S D I I N C C I O I E R A L
H G E Y K K E G T D K C Y U V T M I I F
C G L Y S N N K U L F A T M O Y J A C T
K A Y W O I T X R Y Z C Z F C H W T E H
F C C I C X N J N X S U H Y A T F E R N
D L N H Q T D E Z L L F J K T T M D P K
X I W T E J H R W F G F S K I L H B E W
P M A L E V O L E N T E M V V C Z O D L
P E R S I S T E N T Y D P Z E J L Z M W
```

A feather-like form, structure, or object (5)
An act done to show repentance for a wrong doing (7)
Ashamed; embarrassed (7)
Attentive; full of desire; eager (10)
Balance (11)
Bargained; argued over terms (7)
Became used to a condition (10)
Belittling; making less of something (12)
Bendable (6)
Completely filled or satisfied (5)
Conspiring; plotting; pretending ignorance of a wrong (9)
Doubtful (7)
Elaborately (8)
Enthusiasm (4)
Harsh to the taste or smell (5)
Hold back; suppress; repress (6)
Hole where things can be hidden (5)
In a manner preoccupied by unwholesome matters (8)
Made very angry (10)
Malicious; evil; wishing harm to others (10)

Not talkative (8)
Pushed as if using a lever (7)
Puzzled; perplexed; confused (7)
Quality of not being able to be avoided (13)
Refusing to give up or let go (10)
Removed soluble parts by running through a substance (7)
Restrained by restricting one's arms (8)
Ridicule; scoffing; mocking (8)
Rotten (6)
Skillful (4)
Slapped (6)
Something left over (7)
Sulky; moody (6)
Summoned by using gestures (8)
Teased (7)
Tending to provoke; exciting; stimulating (11)
Tendons (5)
The state or act of looking forward to something (10)
Tired (5)
Understand (6)

When Legends Die Vocabulary Word Search 2 Answer Key

Words are placed backwards, forward, diagonally, up and down. Clues listed below can help you find the words. Circle the hidden vocabulary words in the maze.

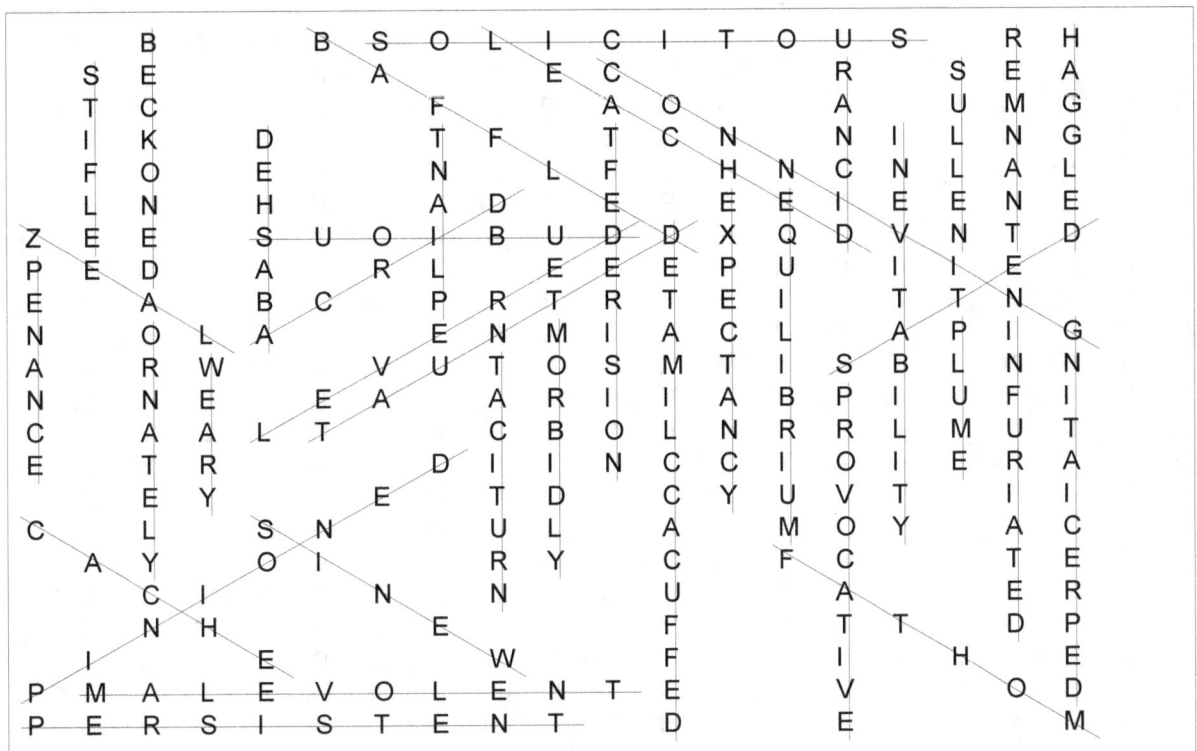

A feather-like form, structure, or object (5)
An act done to show repentance for a wrong doing (7)
Ashamed; embarrassed (7)
Attentive; full of desire; eager (10)
Balance (11)
Bargained; argued over terms (7)
Became used to a condition (10)
Belittling; making less of something (12)
Bendable (6)
Completely filled or satisfied (5)
Conspiring; plotting; pretending ignorance of a wrong (9)
Doubtful (7)
Elaborately (8)
Enthusiasm (4)
Harsh to the taste or smell (5)
Hold back; suppress; repress (6)
Hole where things can be hidden (5)
In a manner preoccupied by unwholesome matters (8)
Made very angry (10)
Malicious; evil; wishing harm to others (10)

Not talkative (8)
Pushed as if using a lever (7)
Puzzled; perplexed; confused (7)
Quality of not being able to be avoided (13)
Refusing to give up or let go (10)
Removed soluble parts by running through a substance (7)
Restrained by restricting one's arms (8)
Ridicule; scoffing; mocking (8)
Rotten (6)
Skillful (4)
Slapped (6)
Something left over (7)
Sulky; moody (6)
Summoned by using gestures (8)
Teased (7)
Tending to provoke; exciting; stimulating (11)
Tendons (5)
The state or act of looking forward to something (10)
Tired (5)
Understand (6)

When Legends Die Vocabulary Word Search 3

Words are placed backwards, forward, diagonally, up and down. Words listed below are included in the maze. Circle the hidden vocabulary words in the maze.

```
A I N E V I T A B I L I T Y F M P W L W
C D I S C O N S O L A T E I D E E X J X
C V Q Q P M T S M H G O N J M X R F M T
L F D H H A D T W K Z F R T L P S R O N
I W W W G L P F K B U D M N E E I V R Q
M D Z B J E M N L R N E W T A C S S B M
A L E Q K V Z V I G B T K C C T T S I K
T L L P B O G A G K R N V Y H A E D D W
E K P N R L T D G H F U R Z E N N L L C
D P L U M E Q D E H S A B A D C T S Y V
P N E M D N C H W R E T T V P Y H T S M
V L V S T T C I Z W I A F H R F F P A S
H T I Y Y A R U A E R S C N O E R E T J
D A T A C N A Y F T A X I R D M E N E C
U C A R N V N L S F I L V O I K M A D N
B I C L Y T C T K X E N J D N D N N E K
I T O P I N I O N E D D G E E D A C R N
O U V B S F D G S J C S L L X B N E E J
U R O B L I N X Y V B L G F D X T G V K
S N R E S T N N H R U G M F C R D V E J
X L P Z K G W E M S A F D A V H P L L S
B E C K O N E D W H R A M B I G U O U S
```

ABASHED	EXPECTANCY	PLIANT
ACCLIMATED	FATHOM	PLUME
ACRID	HAGGLED	PROVOCATIVE
AMBIGUOUS	INEVITABILITY	RANCID
BAFFLED	INFURIATED	REMNANT
BECKONED	LEACHED	SATED
CACHE	LEVERED	SINEW
CUFFED	MALEVOLENT	STIFLE
DEFT	MORBIDLY	SULLEN
DEPRECIATING	ORNATELY	TACITURN
DERISION	PENANCE	TAUNTED
DISCONSOLATE	PERSISTENT	WEARY
DUBIOUS	PINIONED	ZEAL

When Legends Die Vocabulary Word Search 3 Answer Key

Words are placed backwards, forward, diagonally, up and down. Words listed below are included in the maze. Circle the hidden vocabulary words in the maze.

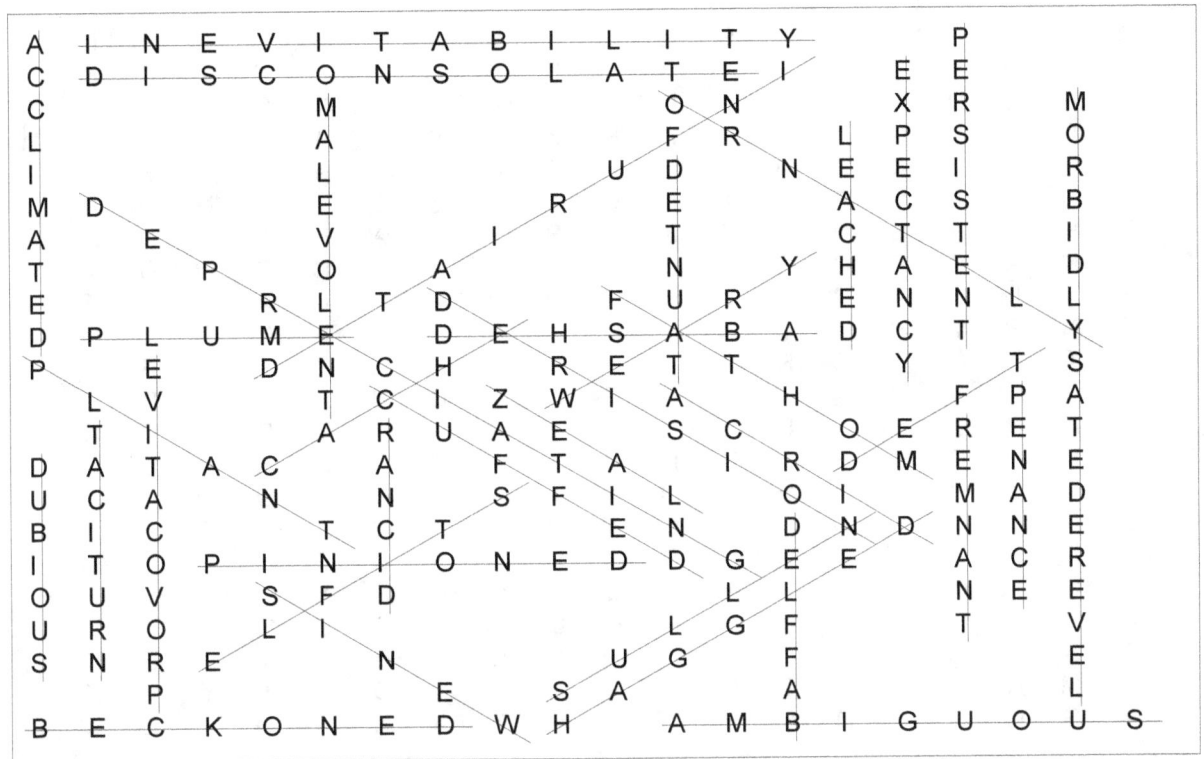

ABASHED	EXPECTANCY	PLIANT
ACCLIMATED	FATHOM	PLUME
ACRID	HAGGLED	PROVOCATIVE
AMBIGUOUS	INEVITABILITY	RANCID
BAFFLED	INFURIATED	REMNANT
BECKONED	LEACHED	SATED
CACHE	LEVERED	SINEW
CUFFED	MALEVOLENT	STIFLE
DEFT	MORBIDLY	SULLEN
DEPRECIATING	ORNATELY	TACITURN
DERISION	PENANCE	TAUNTED
DISCONSOLATE	PERSISTENT	WEARY
DUBIOUS	PINIONED	ZEAL

When Legends Die Vocabulary Word Search 4

Words are placed backwards, forward, diagonally, up and down. Words listed below are included in the maze. Circle the hidden vocabulary words in the maze.

```
B D D I S C O N S O L A T E Y D W G R I
H A W N P O K F Y B V R D K T E N N C N
M X F L D F L Q X B G N R T I T D I G F
J T Q F Y W T I W F R X D Y L A E V W U
M A E S L N Z N C U Q S U W I M H I B R
N U S X A E R T T I Q J B E B I S N W I
N N F N P N D I C J T S I A A L A N K A
P T M A S E C R F D P O O R T C B O D T
Y E V I T A C O V O R P U Y I C A C H E
R D N P T N T B D L A S S V A Y T L B D
L E T A I Z O R A U P G N M E Z C F B Z
W E N L N T M M N P L L C N H I Y V Q
X V A B J C I E S D C S E D I T F E D N
Y E I C Q J E O E K U Y V E S D H M E L
Z Z L J H P D N N O R T E R M M D O T Z
P Q P Q M E O F U E M N R I C Z F R A T
A C R I D K D G L S D L E S U F H B S W
J D S S C X I F M T U D D I F X L I Y S
P M Y E P B B R C P N L W O F Z K D T V
N S B N M G N J D P S D L N E Z J L Z K
Y M M A L E V O L E N T B E D W T Y H K
H A G G L E D S B Y L E T A N R O Z Z Q
```

ABASHED	EXPECTANCY	PLUME
ACCLIMATED	FATHOM	PROVOCATIVE
ACRID	HAGGLED	RANCID
AMBIGUOUS	INEVITABILITY	REMNANT
BAFFLED	INFURIATED	SATED
BECKONED	LEACHED	SINEW
CACHE	LEVERED	SOLICITOUS
CONNIVING	MALEVOLENT	STIFLE
CUFFED	MORBIDLY	SULLEN
DEFT	ORNATELY	TACITURN
DERISION	PENANCE	TAUNTED
DISCONSOLATE	PINIONED	WEARY
DUBIOUS	PLIANT	ZEAL

When Legends Die Vocabulary Word Search 4 Answer Key

Words are placed backwards, forward, diagonally, up and down. Words listed below are included in the maze. Circle the hidden vocabulary words in the maze.

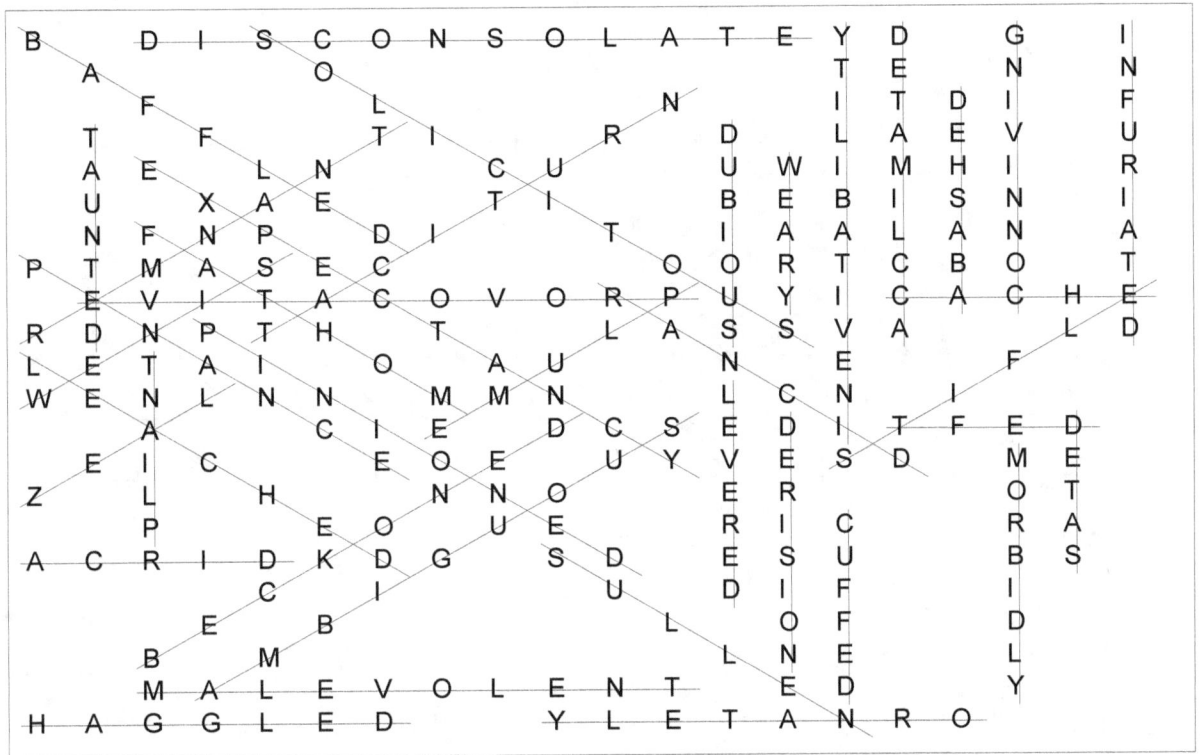

ABASHED	EXPECTANCY	PLUME
ACCLIMATED	FATHOM	PROVOCATIVE
ACRID	HAGGLED	RANCID
AMBIGUOUS	INEVITABILITY	REMNANT
BAFFLED	INFURIATED	SATED
BECKONED	LEACHED	SINEW
CACHE	LEVERED	SOLICITOUS
CONNIVING	MALEVOLENT	STIFLE
CUFFED	MORBIDLY	SULLEN
DEFT	ORNATELY	TACITURN
DERISION	PENANCE	TAUNTED
DISCONSOLATE	PINIONED	WEARY
DUBIOUS	PLIANT	ZEAL

When Legends Die Vocabulary Crossword 1

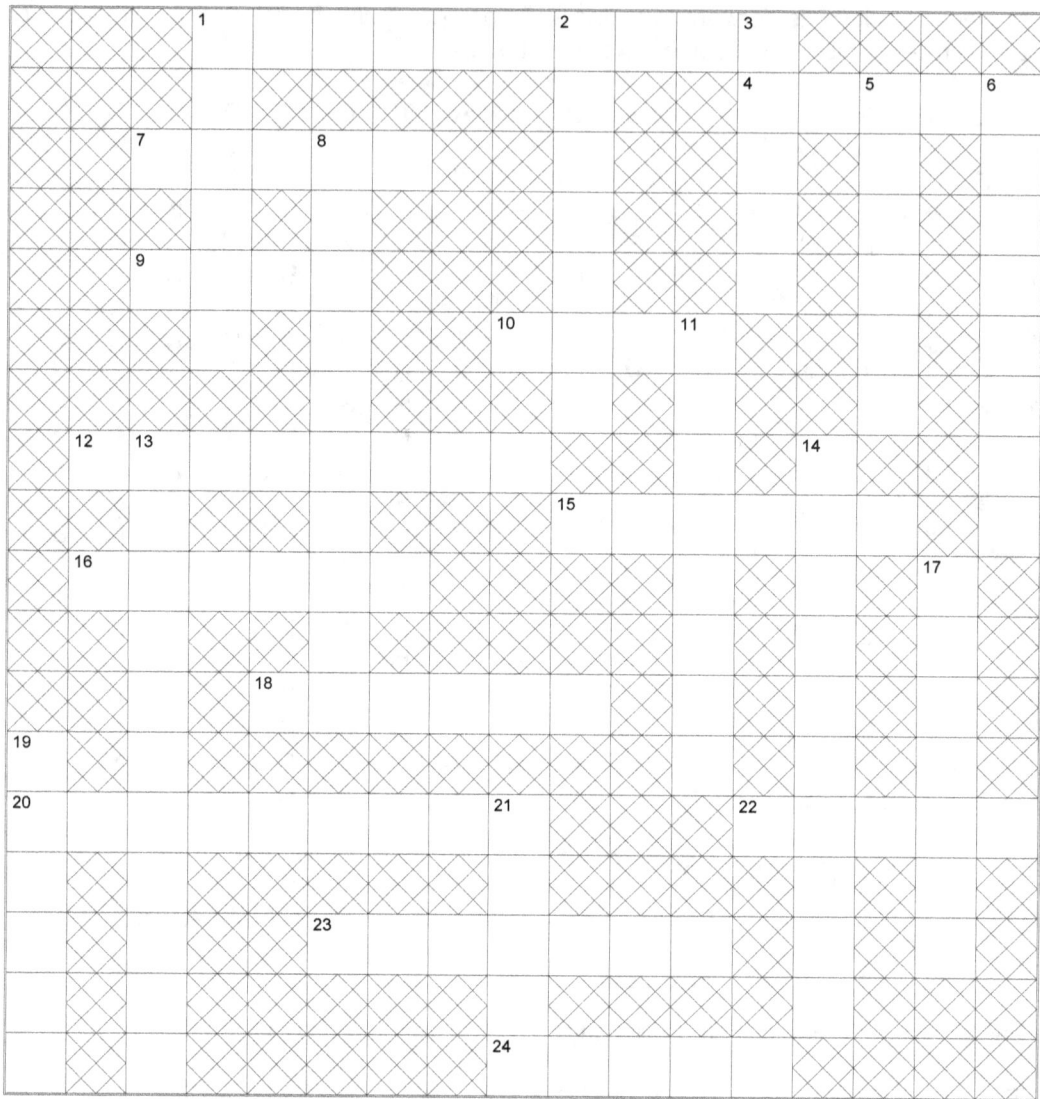

Across
1. Attentive; full of desire; eager
4. Harsh to the taste or smell
7. A feather-like form, structure, or object
9. Enthusiasm
10. Skillful
12. Summoned by using gestures
15. Bendable
16. Slapped
18. Hold back; suppress; repress
20. Indefinite; open to several interpretations
22. Hole where things can be hidden
23. Something left over
24. Tired

Down
1. Sulky; moody
2. Teased
3. Completely filled or satisfied
5. Rotten
6. Ridicule; scoffing; mocking
8. Malicious; evil; wishing harm to others
11. Not talkative
13. Balance
14. Made very angry
17. Ashamed; embarrassed
19. Understand
21. Tendons

When Legends Die Vocabulary Crossword 1 Answer Key

			1					2		3			
			S	O	L	I	C	I	T	O	U	S			
									A		4		5		6
			U								A	C	R	I	D
		7		8											
		P	L	U	M	E			U		T		A		E
			L		A				N		E		N		R
		9													
		Z	E	A	L				T		D		C		I
			N		E		10			11					
							D	E	F	T			I		S
					V				D	A			D		I
	12	13										14			
	B	E	C	K	O	N	E	D		C		I		O
		Q			L		15							
							P	L	I	A	N	T		N
	16												17	
	C	U	F	F	E	D			T		F		A	
		I			N				U		U		B	
				18										
		L		S	T	I	F	L	E		R		A	
19														
F		I							N		I		S	
20							21			22				
A	M	B	I	G	U	O	U	S		C	A	C	H	E
T		R					I			T		E		
H		I		23										
				R	E	M	N	A	N	T		E		D
O		U					E					D		
M		M					24							
							W	E	A	R	Y			

Across
1. Attentive; full of desire; eager
4. Harsh to the taste or smell
7. A feather-like form, structure, or object
9. Enthusiasm
10. Skillful
12. Summoned by using gestures
15. Bendable
16. Slapped
18. Hold back; suppress; repress
20. Indefinite; open to several interpretations
22. Hole where things can be hidden
23. Something left over
24. Tired

Down
1. Sulky; moody
2. Teased
3. Completely filled or satisfied
5. Rotten
6. Ridicule; scoffing; mocking
8. Malicious; evil; wishing harm to others
11. Not talkative
13. Balance
14. Made very angry
17. Ashamed; embarrassed
19. Understand
21. Tendons

When Legends Die Vocabulary Crossword 2

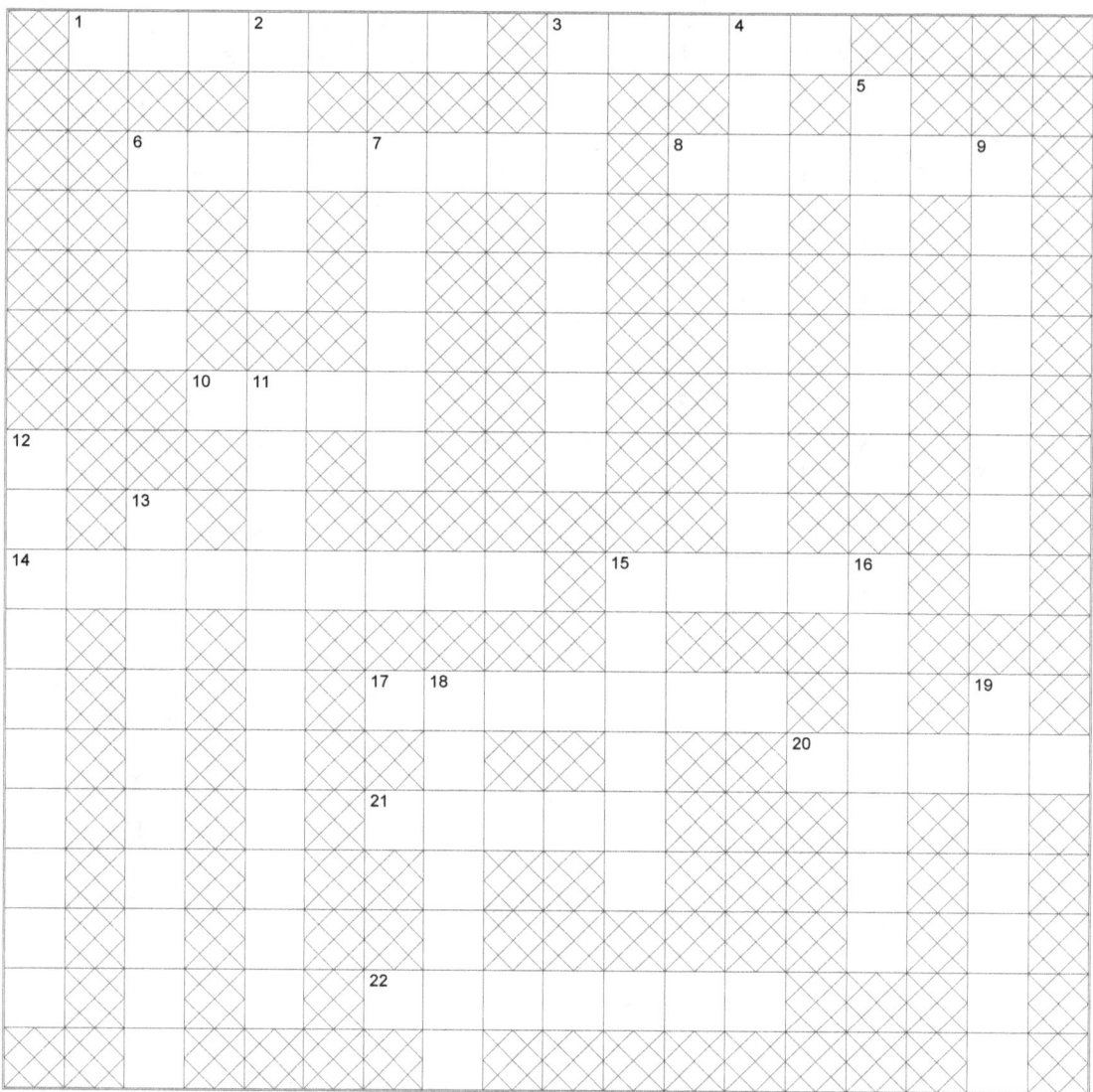

Across
1. An act done to show repentance for a wrong doing
3. A feather-like form, structure, or object
6. Ridicule; scoffing; mocking
8. Bendable
10. Enthusiasm
14. Conspiring; plotting; pretending ignorance of a wrong
15. Completely filled or satisfied
17. Bargained; argued over terms
20. Tendons
21. Hole where things can be hidden
22. Removed soluble parts by running through a substance

Down
2. Harsh to the taste or smell
3. Restrained by restricting one's arms
4. Malicious; evil; wishing harm to others
5. Teased
6. Skillful
7. Hold back; suppress; repress
9. Not talkative
11. Balance
12. Became used to a condition
13. Made very angry
15. Sulky; moody
16. Doubtful
18. Ashamed; embarrassed
19. Something left over

When Legends Die Vocabulary Crossword 2 Answer Key

	1 P	E	N	2 A	N	C	E		3 P	L	4 M	E		
				C					I		A		5 T	
		6 D	E	R	7 S	I	O	N		8 P	L	I	A	N	9 T
		E		I	T					L		E	U		A
		F		D	I					E		V	N		C
		T			F					V		O	T		I
			10 Z	11 E	A	L				E		L	E		T
12 A				Q		E				D		E	D		U
C		13 I		U								N			R
14 C	O	N	N	I	V	I	N	G		15 S	A	T	16 E		N
L		F		L						U			U		
I		U		I		17 H	18 A	G	G	L	E	D	B		19 R
M		R		B			B			L		20 S	I	N	E	W
A		I				21 C	A	C	H	E			O		M
T		A		R			S			N			U		N
E		T		I			H						S		A
D		E		U		22 L	E	A	C	H	E	D			N
		D		M			D								T

Across
1. An act done to show repentance for a wrong doing
3. A feather-like form, structure, or object
6. Ridicule; scoffing; mocking
8. Bendable
10. Enthusiasm
14. Conspiring; plotting; pretending ignorance of a wrong
15. Completely filled or satisfied
17. Bargained; argued over terms
20. Tendons
21. Hole where things can be hidden
22. Removed soluble parts by running through a substance

Down
2. Harsh to the taste or smell
3. Restrained by restricting one's arms
4. Malicious; evil; wishing harm to others
5. Teased
6. Skillful
7. Hold back; suppress; repress
9. Not talkative
11. Balance
12. Became used to a condition
13. Made very angry
15. Sulky; moody
16. Doubtful
18. Ashamed; embarrassed
19. Something left over

When Legends Die Vocabulary Crossword 3

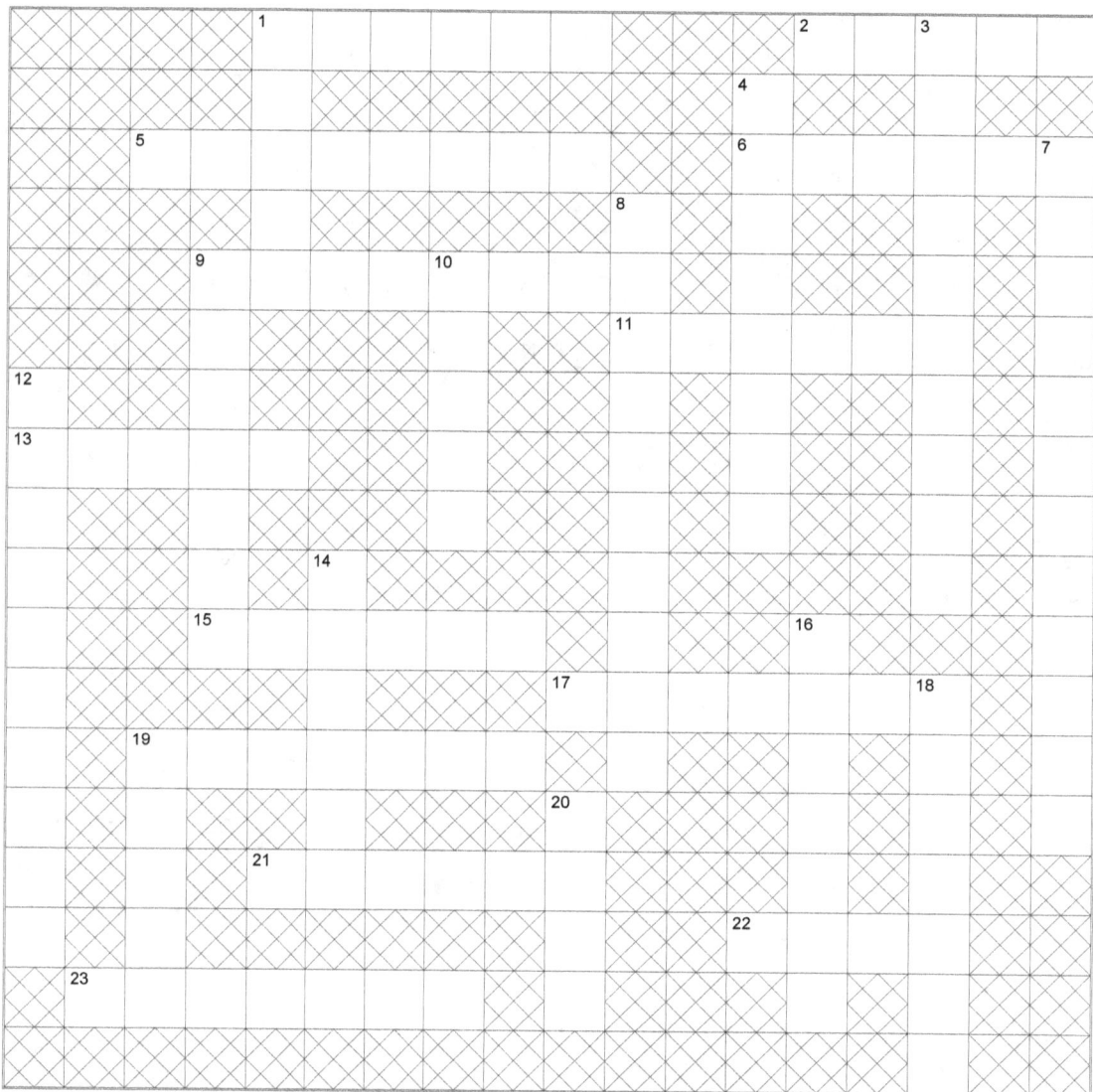

Across
1. Slapped
2. Tired
5. Not talkative
6. Rotten
9. Ridicule; scoffing; mocking
11. Understand
13. Harsh to the taste or smell
15. Sulky; moody
17. Something left over
19. An act done to show repentance for a wrong doing
21. Hold back; suppress; repress
22. Skillful
23. Pushed as if using a lever

Down
1. Hole where things can be hidden
3. Became used to a condition
4. Elaborately
7. Belittling; making less of something
8. Made very angry
9. Doubtful
10. Completely filled or satisfied
12. Malicious; evil; wishing harm to others
14. Bendable
16. Bargained; argued over terms
18. Teased
19. A feather-like form, structure, or object
20. Enthusiasm

When Legends Die Vocabulary Crossword 3 Answer Key

Across
1. Slapped
2. Tired
5. Not talkative
6. Rotten
9. Ridicule; scoffing; mocking
11. Understand
13. Harsh to the taste or smell
15. Sulky; moody
17. Something left over
19. An act done to show repentance for a wrong doing
21. Hold back; suppress; repress
22. Skillful
23. Pushed as if using a lever

Down
1. Hole where things can be hidden
3. Became used to a condition
4. Elaborately
7. Belittling; making less of something
8. Made very angry
9. Doubtful
10. Completely filled or satisfied
12. Malicious; evil; wishing harm to others
14. Bendable
16. Bargained; argued over terms
18. Teased
19. A feather-like form, structure, or object
20. Enthusiasm

When Legends Die Vocabulary Crossword 4

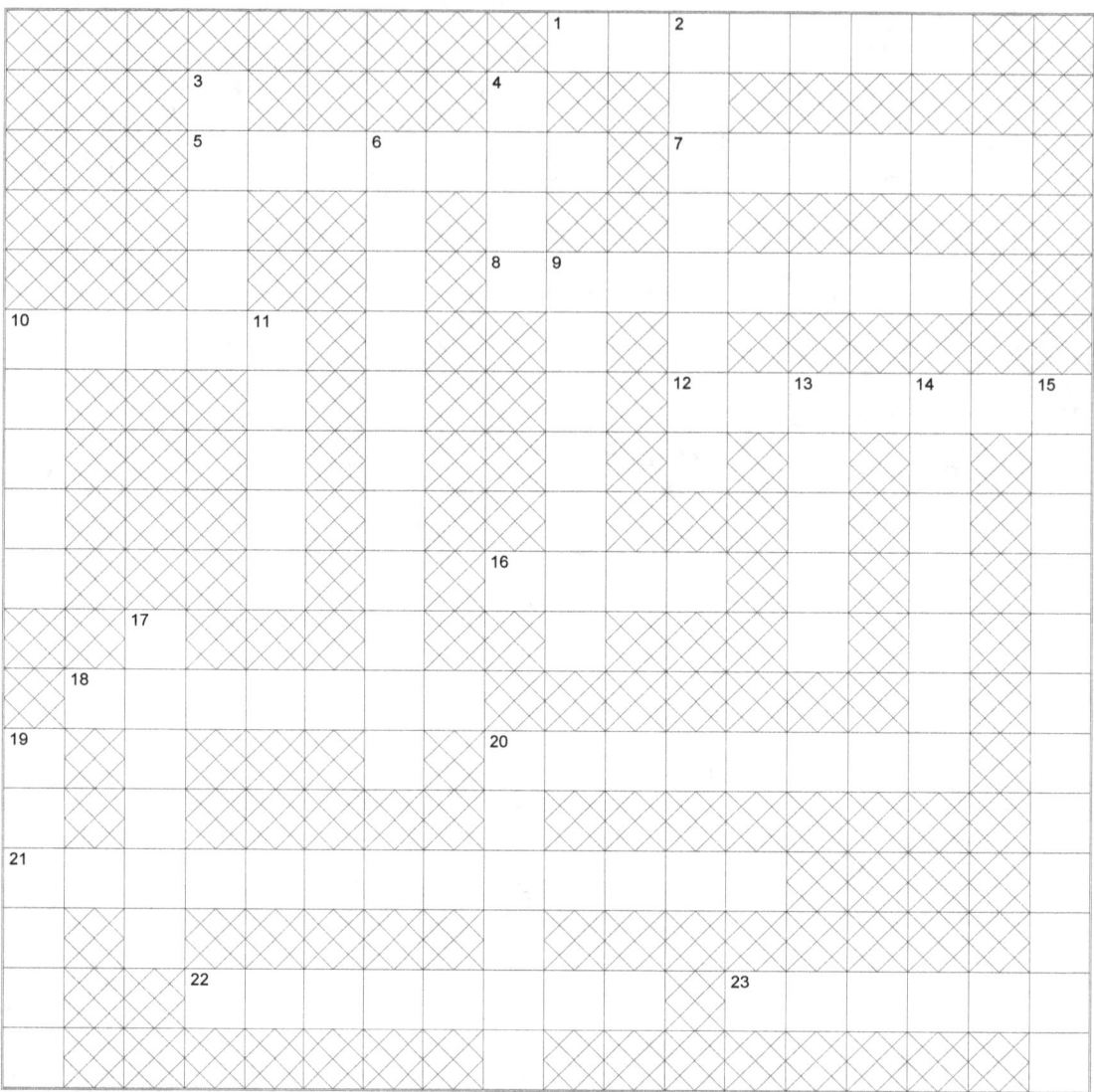

Across
1. Something left over
5. Pushed as if using a lever
7. Rotten
8. Not talkative
10. Tendons
12. Removed soluble parts by running through a substance
16. Enthusiasm
18. Doubtful
20. Restrained by restricting one's arms
21. Quality of not being able to be avoided
22. Summoned by using gestures
23. Sulky; moody

Down
2. In a manner preoccupied by unwholesome matters
3. A feather-like form, structure, or object
4. Skillful
6. Balance
9. Ashamed; embarrassed
10. Completely filled or satisfied
11. Tired
13. Harsh to the taste or smell
14. Bargained; argued over terms
15. Belittling; making less of something
17. Slapped
19. Hold back; suppress; repress
20. Bendable

When Legends Die Vocabulary Crossword 4 Answer Key

Across
1. Something left over
5. Pushed as if using a lever
7. Rotten
8. Not talkative
10. Tendons
12. Removed soluble parts by running through a substance
16. Enthusiasm
18. Doubtful
20. Restrained by restricting one's arms
21. Quality of not being able to be avoided
22. Summoned by using gestures
23. Sulky; moody

Down
2. In a manner preoccupied by unwholesome matters
3. A feather-like form, structure, or object
4. Skillful
6. Balance
9. Ashamed; embarrassed
10. Completely filled or satisfied
11. Tired
13. Harsh to the taste or smell
14. Bargained; argued over terms
15. Belittling; making less of something
17. Slapped
19. Hold back; suppress; repress
20. Bendable

When Legends Die Vocabulary Juggle Letters 1

1. NTTIUARC = 1. _____
   Not talkative

2. IRLYBODM = 2. _____
   In a manner preoccupied by unwholesome matters

3. ESOTDCALOISN = 3. _____
   Gloomy; hopelessly sad

4. UFETNDARII = 4. _____
   Made very angry

5. ALECEDH = 5. _____
   Removed soluble parts by running through a substance

6. ECCAH = 6. _____
   Hole where things can be hidden

7. FDUEFC = 7. _____
   Slapped

8. REDVLEE = 8. _____
   Pushed as if using a lever

9. TISOLICOUS = 9. _____
   Attentive; full of desire; eager

10. UBUGAMOSI =10. _____
    Indefinite; open to several interpretations

11. LTAPIN =11. _____
    Bendable

12. ANLOTERY =12. _____
    Elaborately

13. FAFBDLE =13. _____
    Puzzled; perplexed; confused

14. TDFE =14. _____
    Skillful

15. YRAEW =15. _____
    Tired

When Legends Die Vocabulary Juggle Letters 1 Answer Key

1. NTTIUARC = 1. TACITURN
   Not talkative

2. IRLYBODM = 2. MORBIDLY
   In a manner preoccupied by unwholesome matters

3. ESOTDCALOISN = 3. DISCONSOLATE
   Gloomy; hopelessly sad

4. UFETNDARII = 4. INFURIATED
   Made very angry

5. ALECEDH = 5. LEACHED
   Removed soluble parts by running through a substance

6. ECCAH = 6. CACHE
   Hole where things can be hidden

7. FDUEFC = 7. CUFFED
   Slapped

8. REDVLEE = 8. LEVERED
   Pushed as if using a lever

9. TISOLICOUS = 9. SOLICITOUS
   Attentive; full of desire; eager

10. UBUGAMOSI = 10. AMBIGUOUS
    Indefinite; open to several interpretations

11. LTAPIN = 11. PLIANT
    Bendable

12. ANLOTERY = 12. ORNATELY
    Elaborately

13. FAFBDLE = 13. BAFFLED
    Puzzled; perplexed; confused

14. TDFE = 14. DEFT
    Skillful

15. YRAEW = 15. WEARY
    Tired

When Legends Die Vocabulary Juggle Letters 2

1. LORTYENA = 1. _____
   Elaborately

2. NLLUES = 2. _____
   Sulky; moody

3. OSIITSUOCL = 3. _____
   Attentive; full of desire; eager

4. CEANNPE = 4. _____
   An act done to show repentance for a wrong doing

5. IRTCUANT = 5. _____
   Not talkative

6. ELZA = 6. _____
   Enthusiasm

7. DOILRYMB = 7. _____
   In a manner preoccupied by unwholesome matters

8. DTNEUAT = 8. _____
   Teased

9. IFRNETIUDA = 9. _____
   Made very angry

10. UMLEP = 10. _____
    A feather-like form, structure, or object

11. ECCAH = 11. _____
    Hole where things can be hidden

12. ATFOMH = 12. _____
    Understand

13. EHAGDLG = 13. _____
    Bargained; argued over terms

14. NSIEIDRO = 14. _____
    Ridicule; scoffing; mocking

15. TOPORAVVCIE = 15. _____
    Tending to provoke; exciting; stimulating

When Legends Die Vocabulary Juggle Letters 2 Answer Key

1. LORTYENA = 1. ORNATELY
Elaborately

2. NLLUES = 2. SULLEN
Sulky; moody

3. OSIITSUOCL = 3. SOLICITOUS
Attentive; full of desire; eager

4. CEANNPE = 4. PENANCE
An act done to show repentance for a wrong doing

5. IRTCUANT = 5. TACITURN
Not talkative

6. ELZA = 6. ZEAL
Enthusiasm

7. DOILRYMB = 7. MORBIDLY
In a manner preoccupied by unwholesome matters

8. DTNEUAT = 8. TAUNTED
Teased

9. IFRNETIUDA = 9. INFURIATED
Made very angry

10. UMLEP =10. PLUME
A feather-like form, structure, or object

11. ECCAH =11. CACHE
Hole where things can be hidden

12. ATFOMH =12. FATHOM
Understand

13. EHAGDLG =13. HAGGLED
Bargained; argued over terms

14. NSIEIDRO =14. DERISION
Ridicule; scoffing; mocking

15. TOPORAVVCIE =15. PROVOCATIVE
Tending to provoke; exciting; stimulating

When Legends Die Vocabulary Juggle Letters 3

1. HEABDAS = 1. _____
   Ashamed; embarrassed

2. NSIEW = 2. _____
   Tendons

3. OIENSQUNNASIECTL = 3. _____
   Things that don't matter or don't have significance

4. OUISDUB = 4. _____
   Doubtful

5. ISTTESRPNE = 5. _____
   Refusing to give up or let go

6. DIARCN = 6. _____
   Rotten

7. CENAENP = 7. _____
   An act done to show repentance for a wrong doing

8. NBCKEDEO = 8. _____
   Summoned by using gestures

9. CTSISILOUO = 9. _____
   Attentive; full of desire; eager

10. FENDTIIUAR = 10. _____
    Made very angry

11. SERIOIDN = 11. _____
    Ridicule; scoffing; mocking

12. EANRTMN = 12. _____
    Something left over

13. ULEPM = 13. _____
    A feather-like form, structure, or object

14. INCIVGNNO = 14. _____
    Conspiring; plotting; pretending ignorance of a wrong

15. CEEALHD = 15. _____
    Removed soluble parts by running through a substance

When Legends Die Vocabulary Juggle Letters 3 Answer Key

1. HEABDAS = 1. ABASHED
   Ashamed; embarrassed

2. NSIEW = 2. SINEW
   Tendons

3. OIENSQUNNASIECTL = 3. INCONSEQUENTIALS
   Things that don't matter or don't have significance

4. OUISDUB = 4. DUBIOUS
   Doubtful

5. ISTTESRPNE = 5. PERSISTENT
   Refusing to give up or let go

6. DIARCN = 6. RANCID
   Rotten

7. CENAENP = 7. PENANCE
   An act done to show repentance for a wrong doing

8. NBCKEDEO = 8. BECKONED
   Summoned by using gestures

9. CTSISILOUO = 9. SOLICITOUS
   Attentive; full of desire; eager

10. FENDTIIUAR = 10. INFURIATED
    Made very angry

11. SERIOIDN = 11. DERISION
    Ridicule; scoffing; mocking

12. EANRTMN = 12. REMNANT
    Something left over

13. ULEPM = 13. PLUME
    A feather-like form, structure, or object

14. INCIVGNNO = 14. CONNIVING
    Conspiring; plotting; pretending ignorance of a wrong

15. CEEALHD = 15. LEACHED
    Removed soluble parts by running through a substance

When Legends Die Vocabulary Juggle Letters 4

1. CNRPGEIIEADT = 1. _____
   Belittling; making less of something

2. CACTXPEEYN = 2. _____
   The state or act of looking forward to something

3. MEILQIBURIU = 3. _____
   Balance

4. NRLOTYAE = 4. _____
   Elaborately

5. NLELAMOTEV = 5. _____
   Malicious; evil; wishing harm to others

6. VITACOROPEV = 6. _____
   Tending to provoke; exciting; stimulating

7. ENIRISOD = 7. _____
   Ridicule; scoffing; mocking

8. ATEUNDT = 8. _____
   Teased

9. HCACE = 9. _____
   Hole where things can be hidden

10. ITVATLIBYINEI =10. _____
    Quality of not being able to be avoided

11. LUCASSETNNQEIONI =11. _____
    Things that don't matter or don't have significance

12. INCGNNOIV =12. _____
    Conspiring; plotting; pretending ignorance of a wrong

13. NALIPT =13. _____
    Bendable

14. SLDIOONETCAS =14. _____
    Gloomy; hopelessly sad

15. IUACTNRT =15. _____
    Not talkative

When Legends Die Vocabulary Juggle Letters 4 Answer Key

1. CNRPGEIIEADT = 1. DEPRECIATING
   Belittling; making less of something

2. CACTXPEEYN = 2. EXPECTANCY
   The state or act of looking forward to something

3. MEILQIBURIU = 3. EQUILIBRIUM
   Balance

4. NRLOTYAE = 4. ORNATELY
   Elaborately

5. NLELAMOTEV = 5. MALEVOLENT
   Malicious; evil; wishing harm to others

6. VITACOROPEV = 6. PROVOCATIVE
   Tending to provoke; exciting; stimulating

7. ENIRISOD = 7. DERISION
   Ridicule; scoffing; mocking

8. ATEUNDT = 8. TAUNTED
   Teased

9. HCACE = 9. CACHE
   Hole where things can be hidden

10. ITVATLIBYINEI = 10. INEVITABILITY
    Quality of not being able to be avoided

11. LUCASSETNNQEIONI = 11. INCONSEQUENTIALS
    Things that don't matter or don't have significance

12. INCGNNOIV = 12. CONNIVING
    Conspiring; plotting; pretending ignorance of a wrong

13. NALIPT = 13. PLIANT
    Bendable

14. SLDIOONETCAS = 14. DISCONSOLATE
    Gloomy; hopelessly sad

15. IUACTNRT = 15. TACITURN
    Not talkative

ABASHED	Ashamed; embarrassed
ACCLIMATED	Became used to a condition
ACRID	Harsh to the taste or smell
AMBIGUOUS	Indefinite; open to several interpretations
BAFFLED	Puzzled; perplexed; confused
BECKONED	Summoned by using gestures

CACHE	Hole where things can be hidden
CONNIVING	Conspiring; plotting; pretending ignorance of a wrong
CUFFED	Slapped
DEFT	Skillful
DEPRECIATING	Belittling; making less of something
DERISION	Ridicule; scoffing; mocking

DISCONSOLATE	Gloomy; hopelessly sad
DUBIOUS	Doubtful
EQUILIBRIUM	Balance
EXPECTANCY	The state or act of looking forward to something
FATHOM	Understand
HAGGLED	Bargained; argued over terms

INCONSEQUENTIALS	Things that don't matter or don't have significance
INEVITABILITY	Quality of not being able to be avoided
INFURIATED	Made very angry
LEACHED	Removed soluble parts by running through a substance
LEVERED	Pushed as if using a lever
MALEVOLENT	Malicious; evil; wishing harm to others

MORBIDLY	In a manner preoccupied by unwholesome matters
ORNATELY	Elaborately
PENANCE	An act done to show repentance for a wrong doing
PERSISTENT	Refusing to give up or let go
PINIONED	Restrained by restricting one's arms
PLIANT	Bendable

PLUME	A feather-like form, structure, or object
PROVOCATIVE	Tending to provoke; exciting; stimulating
RANCID	Rotten
REMNANT	Something left over
SATED	Completely filled or satisfied
SINEW	Tendons

SOLICITOUS	Attentive; full of desire; eager
STIFLE	Hold back; suppress; repress
SULLEN	Sulky; moody
TACITURN	Not talkative
TAUNTED	Teased
WEARY	Tired

ZEAL	Enthusiasm

When Legends Die Vocabulary

INCONSEQUENTIALS	PINIONED	DEPRECIATING	REMNANT	DUBIOUS
SULLEN	PERSISTENT	PROVOCATIVE	DEFT	INEVITABILITY
STIFLE	CONNIVING	FREE SPACE	TACITURN	SOLICITOUS
MORBIDLY	TAUNTED	SINEW	EXPECTANCY	LEACHED
RANCID	CUFFED	EQUILIBRIUM	FATHOM	ORNATELY

When Legends Die Vocabulary

DERISION	LEVERED	CACHE	AMBIGUOUS	HAGGLED
SATED	ACRID	ZEAL	DISCONSOLATE	WEARY
MALEVOLENT	ABASHED	FREE SPACE	INFURIATED	PLIANT
BAFFLED	ACCLIMATED	PENANCE	ORNATELY	FATHOM
EQUILIBRIUM	CUFFED	RANCID	LEACHED	EXPECTANCY

When Legends Die Vocabulary

HAGGLED	ZEAL	DISCONSOLATE	EQUILIBRIUM	FATHOM
CUFFED	BAFFLED	PLUME	BECKONED	SATED
PINIONED	CONNIVING	FREE SPACE	PENANCE	DERISION
INCONSEQUENTIALS	CACHE	TACITURN	REMNANT	EXPECTANCY
DUBIOUS	RANCID	MALEVOLENT	DEFT	PERSISTENT

When Legends Die Vocabulary

INFURIATED	SOLICITOUS	TAUNTED	WEARY	ABASHED
ORNATELY	INEVITABILITY	AMBIGUOUS	DEPRECIATING	PROVOCATIVE
ACRID	SULLEN	FREE SPACE	SINEW	LEACHED
ACCLIMATED	STIFLE	LEVERED	PERSISTENT	DEFT
MALEVOLENT	RANCID	DUBIOUS	EXPECTANCY	REMNANT

When Legends Die Vocabulary

WEARY	PERSISTENT	INEVITABILITY	SOLICITOUS	DEPRECIATING
BECKONED	SATED	PENANCE	LEACHED	FATHOM
ACCLIMATED	CONNIVING	FREE SPACE	SINEW	PROVOCATIVE
PLUME	PLIANT	SULLEN	DUBIOUS	INCONSEQUENTIALS
BAFFLED	ACRID	DEFT	EQUILIBRIUM	TAUNTED

When Legends Die Vocabulary

ORNATELY	MALEVOLENT	TACITURN	PINIONED	CUFFED
MORBIDLY	EXPECTANCY	DISCONSOLATE	HAGGLED	ZEAL
LEVERED	AMBIGUOUS	FREE SPACE	REMNANT	INFURIATED
RANCID	DERISION	STIFLE	TAUNTED	EQUILIBRIUM
DEFT	ACRID	BAFFLED	INCONSEQUENTIALS	DUBIOUS

When Legends Die Vocabulary

REMNANT	INCONSEQUENTIALS	SATED	PLUME	LEACHED
CACHE	LEVERED	AMBIGUOUS	EQUILIBRIUM	EXPECTANCY
DEFT	DERISION	FREE SPACE	DEPRECIATING	ACRID
CONNIVING	HAGGLED	PENANCE	MALEVOLENT	MORBIDLY
BAFFLED	PINIONED	ACCLIMATED	PERSISTENT	INEVITABILITY

When Legends Die Vocabulary

FATHOM	CUFFED	WEARY	ABASHED	ORNATELY
ZEAL	BECKONED	INFURIATED	DISCONSOLATE	SINEW
RANCID	PROVOCATIVE	FREE SPACE	TAUNTED	TACITURN
PLIANT	STIFLE	DUBIOUS	INEVITABILITY	PERSISTENT
ACCLIMATED	PINIONED	BAFFLED	MORBIDLY	MALEVOLENT

When Legends Die Vocabulary

INEVITABILITY	FATHOM	SINEW	DISCONSOLATE	DERISION
ZEAL	INFURIATED	LEACHED	PLIANT	SULLEN
DEPRECIATING	ORNATELY	FREE SPACE	TAUNTED	CACHE
TACITURN	STIFLE	SATED	PERSISTENT	BAFFLED
DEFT	ACRID	BECKONED	PLUME	CONNIVING

When Legends Die Vocabulary

WEARY	SOLICITOUS	CUFFED	PINIONED	MALEVOLENT
RANCID	INCONSEQUENTIALS	ABASHED	LEVERED	HAGGLED
PROVOCATIVE	MORBIDLY	FREE SPACE	PENANCE	EXPECTANCY
REMNANT	AMBIGUOUS	EQUILIBRIUM	CONNIVING	PLUME
BECKONED	ACRID	DEFT	BAFFLED	PERSISTENT

When Legends Die Vocabulary

SULLEN	EQUILIBRIUM	CACHE	DEFT	PLIANT
TACITURN	RANCID	ACCLIMATED	PENANCE	LEACHED
CONNIVING	PROVOCATIVE	FREE SPACE	WEARY	MORBIDLY
SOLICITOUS	CUFFED	AMBIGUOUS	ZEAL	PERSISTENT
DEPRECIATING	SINEW	DISCONSOLATE	DUBIOUS	LEVERED

When Legends Die Vocabulary

BAFFLED	ORNATELY	ACRID	TAUNTED	FATHOM
BECKONED	MALEVOLENT	STIFLE	REMNANT	PLUME
SATED	INFURIATED	FREE SPACE	EXPECTANCY	DERISION
PINIONED	ABASHED	HAGGLED	LEVERED	DUBIOUS
DISCONSOLATE	SINEW	DEPRECIATING	PERSISTENT	ZEAL

When Legends Die Vocabulary

LEVERED	AMBIGUOUS	CUFFED	WEARY	PLIANT
SATED	SULLEN	PENANCE	BAFFLED	INFURIATED
MALEVOLENT	DEFT	FREE SPACE	TAUNTED	RANCID
FATHOM	SOLICITOUS	TACITURN	ZEAL	SINEW
DISCONSOLATE	REMNANT	PERSISTENT	CONNIVING	LEACHED

When Legends Die Vocabulary

HAGGLED	PROVOCATIVE	ABASHED	DERISION	STIFLE
ORNATELY	PINIONED	EQUILIBRIUM	ACCLIMATED	INEVITABILITY
MORBIDLY	ACRID	FREE SPACE	CACHE	BECKONED
INCONSEQUENTIALS	EXPECTANCY	PLUME	LEACHED	CONNIVING
PERSISTENT	REMNANT	DISCONSOLATE	SINEW	ZEAL

When Legends Die Vocabulary

SATED	ACRID	BECKONED	CUFFED	MORBIDLY
DERISION	ABASHED	STIFLE	DEFT	PERSISTENT
SINEW	EQUILIBRIUM	FREE SPACE	DUBIOUS	PINIONED
RANCID	SOLICITOUS	LEVERED	CONNIVING	TAUNTED
PENANCE	DISCONSOLATE	DEPRECIATING	INFURIATED	INCONSEQUENTIALS

When Legends Die Vocabulary

AMBIGUOUS	MALEVOLENT	PLUME	EXPECTANCY	PLIANT
LEACHED	BAFFLED	REMNANT	INEVITABILITY	WEARY
HAGGLED	TACITURN	FREE SPACE	CACHE	ZEAL
PROVOCATIVE	ACCLIMATED	FATHOM	INCONSEQUENTIALS	INFURIATED
DEPRECIATING	DISCONSOLATE	PENANCE	TAUNTED	CONNIVING

When Legends Die Vocabulary

INCONSEQUENTIALS	SINEW	CONNIVING	BECKONED	EXPECTANCY
PINIONED	MALEVOLENT	ZEAL	SULLEN	REMNANT
INEVITABILITY	LEVERED	FREE SPACE	ACRID	CUFFED
PERSISTENT	DUBIOUS	RANCID	PENANCE	DEFT
INFURIATED	PLIANT	DISCONSOLATE	PLUME	DERISION

When Legends Die Vocabulary

TACITURN	ORNATELY	SOLICITOUS	CACHE	PROVOCATIVE
MORBIDLY	ABASHED	AMBIGUOUS	BAFFLED	WEARY
DEPRECIATING	HAGGLED	FREE SPACE	LEACHED	TAUNTED
SATED	EQUILIBRIUM	STIFLE	DERISION	PLUME
DISCONSOLATE	PLIANT	INFURIATED	DEFT	PENANCE

When Legends Die Vocabulary

EQUILIBRIUM	LEVERED	INEVITABILITY	LEACHED	CACHE
INCONSEQUENTIALS	ZEAL	EXPECTANCY	HAGGLED	BAFFLED
RANCID	SOLICITOUS	FREE SPACE	CONNIVING	PLUME
WEARY	TAUNTED	TACITURN	ABASHED	ORNATELY
FATHOM	PROVOCATIVE	DEPRECIATING	DUBIOUS	SINEW

When Legends Die Vocabulary

DEFT	MALEVOLENT	STIFLE	ACRID	MORBIDLY
INFURIATED	REMNANT	CUFFED	PLIANT	AMBIGUOUS
BECKONED	DERISION	FREE SPACE	ACCLIMATED	PINIONED
PENANCE	DISCONSOLATE	PERSISTENT	SINEW	DUBIOUS
DEPRECIATING	PROVOCATIVE	FATHOM	ORNATELY	ABASHED

When Legends Die Vocabulary

SINEW	DEPRECIATING	DISCONSOLATE	WEARY	TACITURN
DUBIOUS	LEVERED	ABASHED	INEVITABILITY	PENANCE
ORNATELY	SULLEN	FREE SPACE	LEACHED	HAGGLED
TAUNTED	MORBIDLY	PLUME	STIFLE	BECKONED
PROVOCATIVE	EXPECTANCY	CONNIVING	EQUILIBRIUM	RANCID

When Legends Die Vocabulary

ACRID	PINIONED	MALEVOLENT	PLIANT	DERISION
INCONSEQUENTIALS	DEFT	SOLICITOUS	REMNANT	ZEAL
ACCLIMATED	SATED	FREE SPACE	FATHOM	CACHE
PERSISTENT	INFURIATED	AMBIGUOUS	RANCID	EQUILIBRIUM
CONNIVING	EXPECTANCY	PROVOCATIVE	BECKONED	STIFLE

When Legends Die Vocabulary

SATED	LEACHED	PLUME	FATHOM	MORBIDLY
BECKONED	DUBIOUS	CUFFED	ZEAL	AMBIGUOUS
ABASHED	BAFFLED	FREE SPACE	INEVITABILITY	RANCID
TACITURN	ACCLIMATED	TAUNTED	EQUILIBRIUM	STIFLE
HAGGLED	PROVOCATIVE	SULLEN	SOLICITOUS	INCONSEQUENTIALS

When Legends Die Vocabulary

CONNIVING	DERISION	REMNANT	ORNATELY	DEFT
PLIANT	LEVERED	DISCONSOLATE	INFURIATED	SINEW
WEARY	PERSISTENT	FREE SPACE	PENANCE	CACHE
ACRID	MALEVOLENT	PINIONED	INCONSEQUENTIALS	SOLICITOUS
SULLEN	PROVOCATIVE	HAGGLED	STIFLE	EQUILIBRIUM

When Legends Die Vocabulary

CUFFED	PLIANT	INEVITABILITY	DERISION	LEVERED
DISCONSOLATE	PROVOCATIVE	ACCLIMATED	SOLICITOUS	SULLEN
PENANCE	REMNANT	FREE SPACE	ACRID	BECKONED
CACHE	MORBIDLY	ORNATELY	PINIONED	ABASHED
DEFT	HAGGLED	DEPRECIATING	RANCID	WEARY

When Legends Die Vocabulary

TACITURN	CONNIVING	LEACHED	TAUNTED	MALEVOLENT
DUBIOUS	ZEAL	STIFLE	INFURIATED	PERSISTENT
AMBIGUOUS	SINEW	FREE SPACE	INCONSEQUENTIALS	EXPECTANCY
SATED	PLUME	EQUILIBRIUM	WEARY	RANCID
DEPRECIATING	HAGGLED	DEFT	ABASHED	PINIONED

When Legends Die Vocabulary

EQUILIBRIUM	ACCLIMATED	DEFT	PINIONED	PERSISTENT
PLUME	INEVITABILITY	INCONSEQUENTIALS	STIFLE	ORNATELY
TAUNTED	DERISION	FREE SPACE	ABASHED	CUFFED
REMNANT	ZEAL	RANCID	AMBIGUOUS	LEACHED
BAFFLED	PENANCE	TACITURN	CACHE	FATHOM

When Legends Die Vocabulary

WEARY	EXPECTANCY	DISCONSOLATE	DEPRECIATING	MALEVOLENT
PLIANT	INFURIATED	SOLICITOUS	SULLEN	CONNIVING
MORBIDLY	HAGGLED	FREE SPACE	LEVERED	BECKONED
PROVOCATIVE	ACRID	SATED	FATHOM	CACHE
TACITURN	PENANCE	BAFFLED	LEACHED	AMBIGUOUS

When Legends Die Vocabulary

AMBIGUOUS	LEVERED	DERISION	ORNATELY	SATED
EXPECTANCY	MORBIDLY	TAUNTED	ZEAL	MALEVOLENT
HAGGLED	INFURIATED	FREE SPACE	PERSISTENT	ABASHED
REMNANT	WEARY	DEPRECIATING	DISCONSOLATE	FATHOM
DUBIOUS	CUFFED	ACCLIMATED	SULLEN	CONNIVING

When Legends Die Vocabulary

STIFLE	PLUME	DEFT	INEVITABILITY	RANCID
PENANCE	CACHE	TACITURN	EQUILIBRIUM	PROVOCATIVE
INCONSEQUENTIALS	BECKONED	FREE SPACE	ACRID	SOLICITOUS
PINIONED	BAFFLED	LEACHED	CONNIVING	SULLEN
ACCLIMATED	CUFFED	DUBIOUS	FATHOM	DISCONSOLATE

When Legends Die Vocabulary

SOLICITOUS	WEARY	PERSISTENT	PLUME	REMNANT
SULLEN	DISCONSOLATE	PINIONED	PLIANT	PENANCE
ORNATELY	ACRID	FREE SPACE	ZEAL	AMBIGUOUS
EQUILIBRIUM	ABASHED	FATHOM	CUFFED	EXPECTANCY
SATED	STIFLE	HAGGLED	LEACHED	ACCLIMATED

When Legends Die Vocabulary

SINEW	MALEVOLENT	BECKONED	CONNIVING	INCONSEQUENTIALS
RANCID	INEVITABILITY	INFURIATED	DEFT	DERISION
DEPRECIATING	DUBIOUS	FREE SPACE	BAFFLED	TAUNTED
CACHE	MORBIDLY	PROVOCATIVE	ACCLIMATED	LEACHED
HAGGLED	STIFLE	SATED	EXPECTANCY	CUFFED

www.ingramcontent.com/pod-product-compliance
Lightning Source LLC
Chambersburg PA
CBHW081457070526
44586CB00019B/2403